D0000627

FIFTY REASONS WHY
JESUS CAME TO DIE

BOOKS BY JOHN PIPER

FIFTY REASONS WHY
JESUS CAME TO DIE

JOHN PIPER

CROSSWAY

WHEATON, ILLINOIS

Fifty Reasons Why Jesus Came to Die

Formerly published as *The Passion of Jesus Christ*

Copyright © 2006 by Desiring God Foundation

Published by Crossway
　　　　　　1300 Crescent Street
　　　　　　Wheaton, Illinois

All rights reserved. No part of this publication may be reproduced, stored in a retrieval system or transmitted in any form by any means, electronic, mechanical, photocopy, recording or otherwise, without the prior permission of the publisher, except as provided by USA copyright law.

Italics in biblical quotations indicate emphasis added.

Unless otherwise indicated, Scripture quotations are taken from the ESV® Bible (*The Holy Bible: English Standard Version*®). Copyright © 2001 by Crossway. Used by permission. All rights reserved.

Cover design: Josh Dennis

Cover photo: iStock

First printing, 2006

Printed in the United States of America

Library of Congress Cataloging-in-Publication Data
Piper, John, 1946-
　　Fifty reasons why Jesus came to die / John Piper.
　　　　p. cm.
　　ISBN 13: 978-1-58134-788-3
　　ISBN 10: 1-58134-788-X (TPB : alk. paper)
　　1. Jesus Christ—Passion. I. Title.
BT431.3.P57　　2006
232.96—dc22　　　　　　　　　　　　　　　　　　2003026596

Crossway is a publishing ministry of Good News Publishers.
BP　　　　　12　20　19　18　17　16　15　14　13　12
18　　17　　16　　15　　14　　13　　12　　11　　10　　9

TO
Jesus Christ

Despised and rejected by men;
a man of sorrows, and acquainted with grief . . .
we esteemed him stricken, smitten by God, and afflicted.
But he was wounded for our transgressions;
he was crushed for our iniquities;
upon him was the chastisement that brought us peace,
and with his stripes we are healed.

All we like sheep have gone astray;
we have turned every one to his own way;
and the LORD has laid on him the iniquity of us all.

He was oppressed, and he was afflicted,
yet he opened not his mouth;
like a lamb that is led to the slaughter,
and like a sheep that before its shearers is silent,
so he opened not his mouth. . . .

He was cut off out of the land of the living,
stricken for the transgression of my people. . . .
There was no deceit in his mouth.
Yet it was the will of the LORD to crush him;
he has put him to grief.

THE PROPHET ISAIAH
CHAPTER 53, VERSES 3-10

CONTENTS

CHRIST AND THE CONCENTRATION CAMPS

The most important question of the twenty-first century is: Why did Jesus Christ come and die? To see this importance we must look beyond human causes. The ultimate answer to the question, Who killed Jesus? is: God did. It is a staggering thought. Jesus was his Son! But the whole message of the Bible leads to this conclusion.

GOD MEANT IT FOR GOOD

The Hebrew prophet Isaiah, centuries before Christ, said, "It was the will of the LORD to crush him; he has put him to grief" (Isaiah 53:10). The Christian New Testament says, "[God] did not spare his own Son but gave him up for us all" (Romans 8:32). "God put [Christ] forward . . . by his blood, to be received by faith" (Romans 3:25).

But how does this divine act relate to the horribly sinful actions of the men who killed Jesus? The answer given in the Bible is expressed in an early prayer: "There were gathered together against your holy servant Jesus . . . both Herod and Pontius Pilate, along with the Gentiles and the peoples of Israel, to do whatever your hand and your plan had predestined to take place" (Acts

4:27-28). The scope of this divine sovereignty takes our breath away. But it is also the key to our salvation. God planned it, and by the means of wicked men, he accomplished it. To paraphrase a word from the Jewish Torah: They meant it for evil, but God meant it for good (Genesis 50:20).

And since God meant it for good, we must look beyond human causes to the divine purpose. The central issue of Jesus' death is not the cause, but the purpose—the meaning. Human beings may have their reasons for wanting Jesus out of the way. But only God can design it for the good of the world. In fact, God's purposes for the world in the death of Jesus are unfathomable. I will try to describe fifty of them, but there will always be more to say. My aim is to let the Bible speak. This is where we hear the word of God. I hope that these pointers will set you on a quest to know more and more of God's great design in the death of his Son.

JESUS' DEATH WAS ABSOLUTELY UNIQUE

Why was the death of Jesus so powerful? He was convicted and condemned as a pretender to the throne of Rome. But in the next three centuries his death unleashed a power to suffer and to love that transformed the Roman Empire, and to this day is shaping the world. The answer is that the death of Jesus was absolutely unique. And his resurrection from the dead three days later was an act of God to vindicate what his death achieved.

His death was unique because he was more than a mere human. Not less. He was, as the ancient Nicene Creed says, "very God of very God." This is the testimony of those who knew him and were inspired by him to explain who he is. The apostle John referred to Christ as "the Word" and wrote, "In the beginning was the Word, and the Word was with God, and the

Word was God. . . . And the Word became flesh and dwelt among us" (John 1:1-2, 14).

Moreover he was utterly innocent in his suffering. Not just innocent of the charge of blasphemy, but of all sin. One of his closest disciples said, "He committed no sin, neither was deceit found in his mouth" (1 Peter 2:22). Add to this the fact that he embraced his own death with absolute authority. One of the most stunning statements Jesus ever made was about his own death and resurrection: "I lay down my life that I may take it up again. No one takes it from me, but I lay it down of my own accord. I have authority to lay it down, and I have authority to take it up again" (John 10:17-18). The controversy about which humans killed Jesus is marginal. He chose to die. His heavenly Father ordained it. He embraced it.

The Purpose of His Death Was
Vindicated by the Resurrection

God raised Jesus from the dead to show that he was in the right and to vindicate all his claims. It happened three days later. Early Sunday morning he rose from the dead. He appeared numerous times to his disciples for forty days before his ascension to heaven (Acts 1:3).

The disciples were slow to believe that it really happened. They were not gullible. They were down-to-earth tradesmen. They knew people did not rise from the dead. At one point Jesus insisted on eating fish to prove to them that he was not a ghost (Luke 24:39-43). This was not the resuscitation of a corpse. It was the resurrection of the God-man into an indestructible new life. The early church acclaimed him Lord of heaven and earth. Jesus had finished the work God gave him to do, and the resurrection was the proof that God was satisfied. This book is about what Jesus' death accomplished for the world.

THE DEATH OF CHRIST AND THE CAMPS OF DEATH

It is a tragedy that the story of Christ's death has produced anti-Semitism against Jews and crusading violence against Muslims. We Christians are ashamed of many of our ancestors who did not act in the spirit of Christ. No doubt there are traces of this plague in our own souls. But true Christianity—which is radically different from Western culture, and may not be found in many Christian churches—renounces the advance of religion by means of violence. "My kingdom is not of this world," Jesus said. "If my kingdom were of this world, my servants would have been fighting" (John 18:36). The way of the cross is the way of suffering. Christians are called to die, not kill, in order to show the world how they are loved by Christ.

True Christian love humbly and boldly commends Christ, no matter what it costs, to all peoples as the only saving way to God. Jesus said, "I am the way, and the truth, and the life. No one comes to the Father except through me" (John 14:6). But let it be crystal-clear: To humiliate or scorn or despise or persecute with prideful putdowns or pogroms or crusades or concentration camps is *not* Christian. These were and are, very simply and horribly, disobedience to Jesus Christ. Unlike many of his so-called followers after him, he prayed from the cross, "Father, forgive them, for they know not what they do" (Luke 23:34).

The death of Jesus Christ is the most important event in history, and the most explosive political and personal issue of the twenty-first century. The denial that Christ was crucified is like the denial of the Holocaust. For some it's simply too horrific to affirm.

For others it's an elaborate conspiracy to coerce religious sympathy. But the deniers live in a historical dreamworld. Jesus Christ suffered unspeakably and died. So did Jews.

I am not the first to link Calvary and the concentration camps—the suffering of Jesus Christ and the suffering of Jewish people. In his heart-wrenching, innocence-shattering, mouth-shutting book *Night*, Elie Wiesel tells of his experience as a teenager with his father in the concentration camps of Auschwitz, Buna, and Buchenwald. There was always the threat of "the selection"—the taking away of the weak to be killed and burned in the ovens.

At one point—and only one—Wiesel links Calvary and the camps. He tells of an old rabbi, Akiba Dumer.

> Akiba Dumer left us, a victim of the selection. Lately, he had wandered among us, his eyes glazed, telling everyone of his weakness: "I can't go on. . . . It's all over. . . ." It was impossible to raise his morale. He didn't listen to what we told him. He could only repeat that all was over for him, that he could no longer keep up the struggle, that he had no strength left, nor faith. Suddenly his eyes would become blank, nothing but two open wounds, two pits of terror.[1]

Then Wiesel makes this provocative comment: "Poor Akiba Dumer, if he could have gone on believing in God, if he could have seen a proof of God in this Calvary, he would not have been taken by the selection."[2] I will not presume to put any words in Elie Wiesel's mouth. I am not sure what he meant. But it presses the question: Why the link between Calvary—the place where Jesus died—and the concentration camp?

When I ask this question, I am not thinking of cause or blame. I am thinking of meaning and hope. Is there a way that Jewish suffering may find, not its cause, but its final meaning in the suffering of Jesus Christ? Is it possible to think, not of Christ's death leading to Auschwitz, but of Auschwitz leading to an understanding of Christ's death? Is the link between Calvary and the camps a link of unfathomable empathy? Perhaps only Jesus, in the end, can know what happened during the "one long night"[3] of Jewish suffering. And perhaps a generation of Jewish people, whose grandparents endured their own noxious crucifixion, will be able, as no others, to grasp what happened to the Son of God at Calvary. I leave it as a question. I do not know.

But this I know: Those alleged "Christians" who built the camps never knew the love that moved Jesus Christ toward Calvary. They never knew the Christ who, instead of killing to save a culture, died to save the world. But there are some Christians—the true Christians—who have seen the meaning of the death of Jesus Christ and have been broken and humbled by his suffering. Could it be that these, perhaps better than many, might be able to see and at least begin to fathom the suffering of Jewish people?

What an irony that Christians have been anti-Semitic! Jesus and all his early followers were Jews. People from every group in Palestine were involved in his crucifixion (not just Jews), and people from every group attempted to stop it (including Jews). God himself was the chief Actor in the death of his Son, so that the main question is not, "Which humans brought about the death of Jesus?" but "What did the death of Jesus bring about for humans—including Jews and Muslims and Buddhists and Hindus and nonreligious secularists—and all people everywhere?"

When all is said and done, the most crucial question is: Why? Why did Jesus come to die? Not why in the sense of *cause*, but why in the sense of *purpose*. What did Christ achieve by his death?

Why did he have to suffer so much? What great thing was happening on Calvary for the world?

That's what the rest of this book is about. I have gathered from the New Testament fifty reasons why Jesus came to die. Not fifty causes, but fifty purposes. Infinitely more important than who killed Jesus is the question: What did God achieve for sinners like us in sending his Son to die?

FIFTY REASONS WHY JESUS CAME TO DIE

TO ABSORB THE WRATH OF GOD

*Christ redeemed us from the curse of the law by becoming a
curse for us—for it is written,
"Cursed is everyone who is hanged on a tree."*

Galatians 3:13

*God put [Christ] forward as a propitiation by his blood,
to be received by faith. This was to show God's righteousness,
because in his divine forbearance he had passed over former sins.*

Romans 3:25

*In this is love, not that we have loved God but that he loved us
and sent his Son to be the propitiation for our sins.*

1 John 4:10

If God were not *just*, there would be no *demand* for his Son to
suffer and die. And if God were not *loving*, there would be no *willingness* for his Son to suffer and die. But God is both just and loving.
Therefore his love is willing to meet the demands of his justice.

God's law demanded, "You shall love the LORD your God with
all your heart and with all your soul and with all your might"
(Deuteronomy 6:5). But we have all loved other things more. This
is what sin is—dishonoring God by preferring other things over
him, and acting on those preferences. Therefore, the Bible says,
"All have sinned and fall short of the glory of God" (Romans
3:23). We glorify what we enjoy most. And it isn't God.

Therefore sin is not small, because it is not against a small Sovereign. The seriousness of an insult rises with the dignity of the one insulted. The Creator of the universe is infinitely worthy of respect and admiration and loyalty. Therefore, failure to love him is not trivial—it is treason. It defames God and destroys human happiness.

Since God is just, he does not sweep these crimes under the rug of the universe. He feels a holy wrath against them. They deserve to be punished, and he has made this clear: "For the wages of sin is death" (Romans 6:23). "The soul who sins shall die" (Ezekiel 18:4).

There is a holy curse hanging over all sin. Not to punish would be unjust. The demeaning of God would be endorsed. A lie would reign at the core of reality. Therefore, God says, "Cursed be everyone who does not abide by all things written in the Book of the Law, and do them" (Galatians 3:10; Deuteronomy 27:26).

But the love of God does not rest with the curse that hangs over all sinful humanity. He is not content to show wrath, no matter how holy it is. Therefore God sends his own Son to absorb his wrath and bear the curse for all who trust him. "Christ redeemed us from the curse of the law by becoming a curse for us" (Galatians 3:13).

This is the meaning of the word "propitiation" in the text quoted above (Romans 3:25). It refers to the removal of God's wrath by providing a substitute. The substitute is provided by God himself. The substitute, Jesus Christ, does not just cancel the wrath; he absorbs it and diverts it from us to himself. God's wrath is just, and it was spent, not withdrawn.

Let us not trifle with God or trivialize his love. We will never stand in awe of being loved by God until we reckon with the seriousness of our sin and the justice of his wrath against us. But when, by grace, we waken to our unworthiness, then we may look at the suffering and death of Christ and say, "In this is love, not that we have loved God but that he loved us and sent his Son to be the [wrath-absorbing] *propitiation* for our sins" (1 John 4:10).

Why Jesus Came to Die:

TO PLEASE HIS HEAVENLY FATHER

Yet it was the will of the LORD to crush him;
he has put him to grief.

Isaiah 53:10

Christ loved us and gave himself up for us,
a fragrant offering and sacrifice to God.

Ephesians 5:2

Jesus did not wrestle his angry Father to the floor of heaven and take the whip out of his hand. He did not force him to be merciful to humanity. His death was not the begrudging consent of God to be lenient to sinners. No, what Jesus did when he suffered and died was the Father's idea. It was a breathtaking strategy, conceived even before creation, as God saw and planned the history of the world. That is why the Bible speaks of God's "purpose and grace, which he gave us in Christ Jesus before the ages began" (2 Timothy 1:9).

Already in the Jewish Scriptures the plan was unfolding. The prophet Isaiah foretold the sufferings of the Messiah, who was to take the place of sinners. He said that the Christ would be "smitten by God" in our place.

Surely he has borne our griefs and carried our sorrows; yet we
esteemed him stricken, smitten by God, and afflicted. But he
was wounded for our transgressions; he was crushed for our

iniquities. . . . All we like sheep have gone astray; we have turned every one to his own way; and the LORD has laid on him the iniquity of us all. (Isaiah 53:4-6)

But what is most astonishing about this substitution of Christ for sinners is that it was God's idea. Christ did not intrude on God's plan to punish sinners. God planned for him to be there. One Old Testament prophet says, "It was the will of the LORD to crush him; he has put him to grief" (Isaiah 53:10).

This explains the paradox of the New Testament. On the one hand, the suffering of Christ is an outpouring of God's wrath because of sin. But on the other hand, Christ's suffering is a beautiful act of submission and obedience to the will of the Father. So Christ cried from the cross, "My God, my God, why have you forsaken me?" (Matthew 27:46). And yet the Bible says that the suffering of Christ was a fragrance to God. "Christ loved us and gave himself up for us, a fragrant offering and sacrifice to God" (Ephesians 5:2).

Oh, that we might worship the terrible wonder of the love of God! It is not sentimental. It is not simple. For our sake God did the impossible: He poured out his wrath on his own Son—the one whose submission made him infinitely unworthy to receive it. Yet the Son's very willingness to receive it was precious in God's sight. The wrath-bearer was infinitely loved.

To Learn Obedience and Be Perfected

*Although he was a son, he learned obedience
through what he suffered.*

Hebrews 5:8

*For it was fitting that he, for whom and by whom all things exist,
in bringing many sons to glory,
should make the founder of their salvation
perfect through suffering.*

Hebrews 2:10

The very book in the Bible that says Christ "learned obedience" through suffering, and that he was "made perfect" through suffering, also says that he was "without sin." "In every respect [Christ] has been tempted as we are, *yet without sin*" (Hebrews 4:15).

This is the consistent teaching of the Bible. Christ was sinless. Although he was the divine Son of God, he was really human, with all our temptations and appetites and physical weaknesses. There was hunger (Matthew 21:18) and anger and grief (Mark 3:5) and pain (Matthew 17:12). But his heart was perfectly in love with God, and he acted consistently with that love: "He committed no sin, neither was deceit found in his mouth" (1 Peter 2:22).

Therefore, when the Bible says that Jesus "learned obedience through what he suffered," it doesn't mean that he learned to stop disobeying. It means that with each new trial he learned in practice—and in pain—what it means to obey. When it says that he was "made perfect through suffering," it doesn't mean that he was gradually getting rid of defects. It means that he was gradually fulfilling the perfect righteousness that he had to have in order to save us.

That's what he said at his baptism. He didn't need to be baptized because he was a sinner. Rather, he explained to John the Baptist, "Thus it is fitting for us to fulfill all righteousness" (Matthew 3:15).

The point is this: *If the Son of God had gone from incarnation to the cross without a life of temptation and pain to test his righteousness and his love, he would not be a suitable Savior for fallen man.* His suffering not only absorbed the wrath of God. It also fulfilled his true humanity and made him able to call us brothers and sisters (Hebrews 2:17).

To Achieve His Own Resurrection from the Dead

Now may the God of peace who brought again from the dead
our Lord Jesus, the great shepherd of the sheep,
by the blood of the eternal covenant,
equip you with everything good that you may do his will.

Hebrews 13:20-21

The death of Christ did not merely precede his resurrection—it was the price that obtained it. That's why Hebrews 13:20 says that God brought him from the dead "by the blood of the eternal covenant."

The "blood of the . . . covenant" is the blood of Jesus. As he said, "This is my blood of the covenant" (Matthew 26:28). When the Bible speaks of the blood of Jesus, it refers to his death. No salvation would be accomplished by the mere bleeding of Jesus. His bleeding *to death* is what makes his blood-shedding crucial.

Now what is the relationship between this shedding of Jesus' blood and the resurrection? The Bible says he was raised not just *after* the blood-shedding, but *by* it. This means that what the death of Christ accomplished was so full and so perfect that the resurrection was the *reward* and *vindication* of Christ's achievement in death.

The wrath of God was satisfied with the suffering and death

of Jesus. The holy curse against sin was fully absorbed. The obedience of Christ was completed to the fullest measure. The price of forgiveness was totally paid. The righteousness of God was completely vindicated. All that was left to accomplish was the public declaration of God's endorsement. This he gave by raising Jesus from the dead.

When the Bible says, "If Christ has not been raised, your faith is futile and you are still in your sins" (1 Corinthians 15:17), the point is not that the resurrection is the price paid for our sins. The point is that the resurrection proves that the death of Jesus is an all-sufficient price. If Jesus did not rise from the dead, then his death was a failure, God did not vindicate his sin-bearing achievement, and we are still in our sins.

But in fact "Christ was raised from the dead by the glory of the Father" (Romans 6:4). The success of his suffering and death was vindicated. And if we put our trust in Christ, we are *not* still in our sins. For "*by* the blood of the eternal covenant," the Great Shepherd has been raised and lives forever.

TO SHOW THE WEALTH OF GOD'S LOVE AND GRACE FOR SINNERS

*One will scarcely die for a righteous person—
though perhaps for a good person one would dare even to die—
but God shows his love for us in that while we were still sinners,
Christ died for us.*

Romans 5:7-8

*For God so loved the world, that he gave his only Son,
that whoever believes in him should not perish but have eternal life.*

John 3:16

*In him we have redemption through his blood,
the forgiveness of our trespasses,
according to the riches of his grace.*

Ephesians 1:7

The measure of God's love for us is shown by two things. One is the degree of his sacrifice in saving us from the penalty of our sin. The other is the degree of unworthiness that we had when he saved us.

We can hear the measure of his sacrifice in the words, "He gave his only son" (John 3:16). We also hear it in the word *Christ.* This is a name based on the Greek title *Christos,* or "Anointed One," or "Messiah." It is a term of great dignity. The Messiah was to be the King of Israel. He would conquer the

Romans and bring peace and security to Israel. Thus the person whom God sent to save sinners was his own divine Son, his *only* Son, and the Anointed King of Israel—indeed the king of the world (Isaiah 9:6-7).

When we add to this consideration the horrific death by crucifixion that Christ endured, it becomes clear that the sacrifice the Father and the Son made was indescribably great—even infinite, when you consider the distance between the divine and the human. But God chose to make this sacrifice to save us.

The measure of his love for us increases still more when we consider our unworthiness. "Perhaps for a good person one would dare even to die—but God shows his love for us in that *while we were still sinners*, Christ died for us" (Romans 5:7-8). We deserved divine punishment, not divine sacrifice.

I have heard it said, "God didn't die for frogs. So he was responding to our value as humans." This turns grace on its head. We are *worse* off than frogs. They have not sinned. They have not rebelled and treated God with the contempt of being inconsequential in their lives. God did not have to die for frogs. They aren't bad enough. We are. Our debt is so great, only a divine sacrifice could pay it.

There is only one explanation for God's sacrifice for us. It is not us. It is "the riches of his grace" (Ephesians 1:7). It is all free. It is not a response to our worth. It is the overflow of his infinite worth. In fact, that is what divine love is in the end: a passion to enthrall undeserving sinners, at great cost, with what will make us supremely happy forever, namely, his infinite beauty.

TO SHOW HIS OWN LOVE FOR US

Christ loved us and gave himself up for us,
a fragrant offering and sacrifice to God.

EPHESIANS 5:2

Christ loved the church and gave himself up for her.

EPHESIANS 5:25

[He] loved me and gave himself for me.

GALATIANS 2:20

The death of Christ is not only the demonstration of *God's* love (John 3:16), it is also the supreme expression of *Christ's own* love for all who receive it as their treasure. The early witnesses who suffered most for being Christians were captured by this fact: Christ "loved me and gave himself for me" (Galatians 2:20). They took the self-giving act of Christ's sacrifice very personally. They said, "He loved *me*. He gave himself for *me*."

Surely this is the way we should understand the sufferings and death of Christ. They have to do with me. They are about Christ's love for me personally. It is *my* sin that cuts me off from God, not sin in general. It is *my* hard-heartedness and spiritual numbness that demean the worth of Christ. I am lost and perishing. When it comes to salvation, I have forfeited all claim on justice. All I can do is plead for mercy.

Then I see Christ suffering and dying. For whom? It says,

"Christ loved the *church* and gave himself up for *her*" (Ephesians 5:25). "Greater love has no one than this, that someone lays down his life for *his friends*" (John 15:13). "The Son of Man came not to be served but to serve, and to give his life as a ransom for *many*" (Matthew 20:28).

And I ask, Am I among the "many"? Can I be one of his "friends"? May I belong to the "church"? And I hear the answer, "Believe in the Lord Jesus, and you will be saved" (Acts 16:31). "Everyone who calls on the name of the Lord will be saved" (Romans 10:13). "Everyone who believes in him receives forgiveness of sins through his name" (Acts 10:43). "To all who did receive him, who believed in his name, he gave the right to become children of God" (John 1:12). "Whoever believes in him should not perish but have eternal life" (John 3:16).

My heart is swayed, and I embrace the beauty and bounty of Christ as my treasure. And there flows into my heart this great reality—the love of Christ for me. So I say with those early witnesses, "He loved me and gave himself for me."

And what do I mean? I mean that he paid the highest price possible to give me the greatest gift possible. And what is that? It is the gift he prayed for at the end of his life: "Father, I desire that they also, whom you have given me, may be with me where I am, to see my glory" (John 17:24). In his suffering and death "we have seen his glory, glory as of the only Son from the Father, full of grace and truth" (John 1:14). We have seen enough to capture us for his cause. But the best is yet to come. He died to secure this for us. That is the love of Christ.

To Cancel the Legal Demands of the Law Against Us

And you, who were dead in your trespasses . . .
God made alive together with him,
having forgiven us all our trespasses,
by canceling the record of debt that stood
against us with its legal demands.
This he set aside, nailing it to the cross.

Colossians 2:13

What a folly it is to think that our good deeds may one day outweigh our bad deeds. It is folly for two reasons.

First, *it is not true*. Even our good deeds are defective, because we don't honor God in the way we do them. Do we do our good deeds in joyful dependence on God with a view to making known his supreme worth? Do we fulfill the overarching command to serve people "by the strength that God supplies—in order that in everything God may be glorified through Jesus Christ" (1 Peter 4:11)?

What then shall we say in response to God's word, "Whatever does not proceed from faith is sin" (Romans 14:23)? I think we shall say nothing. "Whatever the law says it speaks . . . so that every mouth may be stopped" (Romans 3:19). We will say nothing. It is folly to think that our good deeds will outweigh our bad deeds before God. Without Christ-exalting faith, our deeds will signify nothing but rebellion.

The second reason it is folly to hope in good deeds is that *this is not the way God saves*. If we are saved from the consequences of our bad deeds, it will not be because they weighed less than our good deeds. It will be because the "record of [our] debt" in heaven has been nailed to the cross of Christ. God has a totally different way of saving sinners than by weighing their deeds. There is no hope in our deeds. There is only hope in the suffering and death of Christ.

There is no salvation by balancing the records. There is only salvation by canceling records. The record of our bad deeds (including our defective good deeds), along with the just penalties that each deserves, must be blotted out—not balanced. This is what Christ suffered and died to accomplish.

The cancellation happened when the record of our deeds was "nailed to the cross" (Colossians 2:13). How was this damning record nailed to the cross? Parchment was not nailed to the cross. Christ was. So Christ became my damning record of bad (and good) deeds. He endured my damnation. He put my salvation on a totally different footing. He is my only hope. And faith in him is my only way to God.

To Become a Ransom for Many

*The Son of Man came not to be served but to serve,
and to give his life as a ransom for many.*

Mark 10:45

There is no thought in the Bible that Satan had to be paid off to let sinners be saved. What happened to Satan when Christ died was not payment, but defeat. The Son of God became human so "that through death he might destroy the one who has the power of death, that is, the devil" (Hebrews 2:14). There was no negotiation.

When Jesus says that he came "to give his life as a ransom," the focus is not on who gets the payment. The focus is on his own life as the payment, and on his freedom in serving rather than being served, and on the "many" who will benefit from the payment he makes.

If we ask who received the ransom, the biblical answer would surely be God. The Bible says that Christ "gave himself up for us, [an] . . . offering . . . *to God*" (Ephesians 5:2). Christ "offered himself without blemish *to God*" (Hebrews 9:14). The whole need for a substitute to die on our behalf is because we have sinned against *God* and fallen short of the glory of *God* (Romans 3:23). And because of our sin, "the whole world [is] held accountable to *God*" (Romans 3:19). So when Christ gives himself as a ransom for us, the Bible says that we are freed from the condemnation of God. "There is therefore now no condemnation for those who are in Christ Jesus" (Romans 8:1). The ultimate captivity from which we need release is the final "judgment of *God*" (Romans 2:2; Revelation 14:7).

The ransom price of this release from God's condemnation is the life of Christ. Not just his life lived, but his life given up in death. Jesus said repeatedly to his disciples, "The Son of Man is going to be delivered into the hands of men, and they will kill him" (Mark 9:31). In fact, one of the reasons Jesus loved to call himself "the Son of Man" (over sixty-five times in the Gospels) was that it had the ring of mortality about it. Men can die. That's why he had to be one. The ransom could only be paid by the Son of Man, because the ransom was a life given up in death.

The price was not coerced from him. That's the point of saying, "The Son of Man came not to be served but to serve." He needed no service from us. He was the giver, not the receiver. "No one takes [my life] from me, but I lay it down of my own accord" (John 10:18). The price was paid freely; it was not forced. Which brings us again to his love. He freely chose to rescue us at the cost of his life.

How many did Christ effectively ransom from sin? He said that he came "to give his life as a ransom *for many*." Yet not everyone will be ransomed from the wrath of God. But the *offer* is for everyone. "There is one mediator between God and men, the man Christ Jesus, who gave himself as a ransom *for all*" (1 Timothy 2:5-6). No one is excluded from this salvation who embraces the treasure of the ransoming Christ.

FOR THE FORGIVENESS OF OUR SINS

*In him we have redemption through his blood,
the forgiveness of our trespasses.*

Ephesians 1:7

*This is my blood of the covenant,
which is poured out for many
for the forgiveness of sins.*

Matthew 26:28

When we forgive a debt or an offense or an injury, we don't require a payment for settlement. That would be the opposite of forgiveness. If repayment is made to us for what we lost, there is no need for forgiveness. We have our due.

Forgiveness assumes grace. If I am injured by you, grace lets it go. I don't sue you. I forgive you. Grace gives what someone doesn't deserve. That's why *forgiveness* has the word *give* in it. For*give*ness is not "*get*ting" even. It is giving away the right to get even.

That is what God does to us when we trust Christ: "Everyone who believes in him receives forgiveness of sins through his name" (Acts 10:43). If we believe in Christ, God no longer holds our sins against us. This is God's own testimony in the Bible: "I, I am he who wipes out your transgressions for my own sake" (Isaiah 43:25). "As far as the east is from the west, so far does he remove our transgressions from us" (Psalm 103:12).

But this raises a problem. We all know that forgiveness is not enough. We may only see it clearly when the injury is great—like murder or rape. Neither society nor the universe can hold together if judges (or God) simply say to every murderer and rapist, "Are you sorry? Okay. The state forgives you. You may go." In cases like these we see that while a victim may have a forgiving spirit, the state cannot forsake justice.

So it is with God's justice. All sin is serious, because it is against God (see chapter 1). He is the one whose glory is injured when we ignore or disobey or blaspheme him. His justice will no more allow him simply to set us free than a human judge can cancel all the debts that criminals owe to society. The injury done to God's glory by our sin must be repaired so that in justice his glory shines more brightly. And if we criminals are to go free and be forgiven, there must be some dramatic demonstration that the honor of God is upheld even though former blasphemers are being set free.

That is why Christ suffered and died. "In him we have redemption *through his blood*, the forgiveness of our trespasses" (Ephesians 1:7). Forgiveness costs us nothing. All our costly obedience is the fruit, not the root, of being forgiven. That's why we call it grace. But it cost Jesus his life. That is why we call it just. Oh, how precious is the news that God does not hold our sins against us! And how beautiful is Christ, whose blood made it right for God to do this.

TO PROVIDE THE BASIS FOR OUR JUSTIFICATION

We have now been justified by his blood.

ROMANS 5:9

*[We] are justified by his grace as a gift,
through the redemption that is in Christ Jesus.*

ROMANS 3:24

*We hold that one is justified by faith
apart from works of the law.*

ROMANS 3:28

Being justified before God and being forgiven by God are not identical. To be justified in a courtroom is not the same as being forgiven. Being forgiven implies that I am guilty and my crime is not counted. Being justified implies that I have been tried and found innocent. My claim is just. I am vindicated. The *judge* says, "Not guilty."

Justifying is a legal act. It means declaring someone to be just. It is a verdict. The verdict of justification does not *make* a person just. It *declares* a person just. It is based on someone actually being just. We can see this most clearly when the Bible tells us that, in response to Jesus' teaching, the people "justified" *God* (Luke 7:29). This does not mean they *made* God just (since he already was). It means they declared God to be just.

The moral change we undergo when we trust Christ is not justification. The Bible usually calls that sanctification—the process of becoming good. Justification is not that process. It is not a process at all. It is a declaration that happens in a moment. A verdict: Just! Righteous!

The ordinary way to be justified in a human court is to keep the law. In that case the jury and the judge simply declare what is true of you: You kept the law. They justify you. But in the courtroom of God, we have *not* kept the law. Therefore, justification, on ordinary terms, is hopeless. The Bible even says, "He who justifies the wicked [is] an abomination to the LORD" (Proverbs 17:15). And yet, amazingly, because of Christ, it also says God "justifies the ungodly" who trust in his grace (Romans 4:5). God does what looks abominable.

Why is it not abominable? Or, as the Bible puts it, how can God "be just *and* the justifier of the one who [simply!] has faith in Jesus" (Romans 3:26)? It is not abominable for God to justify the ungodly who trust him, for two reasons. One is that *Christ shed his blood to cancel the guilt of our crime.* So it says, "We have now been justified *by his blood*" (Romans 5:9). But that is only the removal of guilt. That does not declare us righteous. Canceling our failures to keep the law is not the same as declaring us to be a law-keeper. When a teacher cancels from the record an exam that got an F, it's not the same as declaring it an A. If the bank were to forgive me the debts on my account, that would not be the same as declaring me rich. So also, canceling our sins is not the same as declaring us righteous. The cancellation must happen. That is essential to justification. But there is more. There is another reason why it is not abominable for God to justify the ungodly by faith. For that we turn to the next chapter.

To Complete the Obedience That Becomes Our Righteousness

*Being found in human form, he humbled himself by becoming
obedient to the point of death, even death on a cross.*

Philippians 2:8

*For as by the one man's disobedience the many were made sinners,
so by the one man's obedience the many will be made righteous.*

Romans 5:19

*For our sake he made him to be sin who knew no sin,
so that in him we might become the righteousness of God.*

2 Corinthians 5:21

*. . . not having a righteousness of my own that comes from the law,
but that which comes through faith in Christ.*

Philippians 3:9

Justification is not merely the cancellation of my unrighteousness. It is also the imputation of Christ's righteousness to me. I do not have a righteousness that commends me to God. My claim before God is this: "not having a righteousness of my own that comes from the law, but that which comes through faith in Christ" (Philippians 3:9).

This is Christ's righteousness. It is imputed to me. That means Christ fulfilled all righteousness perfectly; and then that righteousness was reckoned to be mine, when I trusted in him. I was counted righteous. God looked on Christ's perfect righteousness, and he declared me to be righteous with the righteousness of Christ.

So there are two reasons why it is not abominable for God to justify the ungodly (Romans 4:5). First, *the death of Christ paid the debt of our unrighteousness* (see the previous chapter). Second, *the obedience of Christ provided the righteousness we needed to be justified in God's court.* The demands of God for entrance into eternal life are not merely that our unrighteousness be canceled, but that our perfect righteousness be established.

The suffering and death of Christ is the basis of both. His suffering is the suffering that our unrighteousness deserved. "He was wounded for our transgressions; he was crushed for our iniquities" (Isaiah 53:5). But his suffering and death were also the climax and completion of the obedience that became the basis of our justification. He was "obedient to the point of death, even death on a cross" (Philippians 2:8). His death was the pinnacle of his obedience. This is what the Bible refers to when it says, "By the one man's obedience the many will be made righteous" (Romans 5:19).

Therefore, Christ's death became the basis of our pardon and our perfection. "For our sake [God] made him to be sin who knew no sin, so that in him we might become the righteousness of God" (2 Corinthians 5:21). What does it mean that God made the sinless Christ to be sin? It means our sin was imputed to him, and thus he became our pardon. And what does it mean that we (who *are* sinners) become the righteousness of God in Christ? It means, similarly, that Christ's righteousness is imputed to us, and thus he became our perfection.

May Christ be honored for his whole achievement in suffering and dying! Both the work of pardoning our sin, and the work of providing our righteousness. Let us admire him and treasure him and trust him for this great achievement.

To Take Away Our Condemnation

Who is to condemn? Christ Jesus is the one who died—
more than that, who was raised—who is at the right hand
of God, who indeed is interceding for us.

Romans 8:34

The great conclusion to the suffering and death of Christ is this: "There is therefore now no condemnation for those who are in Christ Jesus" (Romans 8:1). To be "in Christ" means to be in relationship to him by faith. Faith in Christ unites us to Christ so that his death becomes our death and his perfection becomes our perfection. Christ becomes our punishment (which we don't have to bear) and our perfection (which we cannot perform).

Faith is not the ground of our acceptance with God. Christ alone is. Faith unites us to Christ so that his righteousness is counted as ours. "We know that a person is not justified by works of the law but through faith in Jesus Christ, so we also have believed in Christ Jesus, in order to be justified by faith in Christ and not by works of the law, because by works of the law no one will be justified" (Galatians 2:16). Being "justified by faith" and being "justified . . . in Christ" (Galatians 2:17) are parallel terms. We are in Christ by faith, and therefore justified.

When the question is asked, "Who is to condemn?" the answer is assumed. No one! Then the basis is declared: "Christ Jesus is the one who died!" The death of Christ secures our freedom from condemnation. It is as sure that we cannot be condemned as it is sure that Christ died. There is no double jeopardy in God's court. We will not be condemned twice for the same offenses. Christ has died once for our sins. We will not be condemned for them. Condemnation is gone not because there isn't any, but because it has already happened.

But what about condemnation by the world? Is that not an answer to the question, "Who is to condemn?" Aren't Christians condemned by the world? There have been many martyrs. The answer is that no one can condemn us *successfully*. Charges can be brought, but none will stick in the end. "Who shall bring any charge against God's elect? It is God who justifies" (Romans 8:33). It's the same as when the Bible asks, "Who shall separate us from the love of Christ? Shall tribulation, or distress, or persecution, or famine, or nakedness, or danger, or sword?" (Romans 8:35). The answer is not that these things don't happen to Christians. The answer is: "In all these things we are more than conquerors through him who loved us" (Romans 8:37).

The world will bring its condemnation. They may even put their sword behind it. But we know that the highest court has already ruled in our favor. "If God is for us, who can be against us?" (Romans 8:31). No one successfully. If they reject us, he accepts us. If they hate us, he loves us. If they imprison us, he sets our spirits free. If they afflict us, he refines us by the fire. If they kill us, he makes it a passage to paradise. They cannot defeat us. Christ has died. Christ is risen. We are alive in him. And in him there is no condemnation. We are forgiven, and we are righteous. "And the righteous are bold as a lion" (Proverbs 28:1).

13

To Abolish Circumcision and All Rituals as the Basis of Salvation

*But if I, brothers, still preach circumcision . . .
the offense of the cross has been removed.*
Galatians 5:11

*It is those who want to make a good showing in the flesh
who would force you to be circumcised, and only in order that
they may not be persecuted for the cross of Christ.*
Galatians 6:12

The place of circumcision was a huge controversy in the early church. It had a long, respected, biblical place ever since God commanded it in Genesis 17:10. Christ was a Jew. All his twelve apostles were Jews. Almost all the first converts to Christianity were Jews. The Jewish Scriptures were (and are) part of the Bible of the Christian church. It is not surprising that Jewish rituals would come over into the Christian church.

They came. And with them came controversy. The message of Christ was spreading to non-Jewish cities like Antioch of Syria. Gentiles were believing on Christ. The question became urgent: How did the central truth of the gospel relate to rituals like circumcision? How did rituals relate to the gospel of Christ—the news that, if you believe on him your sins are forgiven, and you are justified before God? God is for you. You have eternal life.

Throughout the Gentile world the apostles were preaching forgiveness and justification by faith alone. Peter preached: "To [Christ] all the prophets bear witness that everyone who believes in him receives *forgiveness of sins* through his name" (Acts 10:43). Paul preached: "Let it be known to you therefore, brothers, that . . . by him everyone who believes is *justified* from everything from which you could not be *justified* by the law of Moses" (Acts 13:38-39, author's translation).

But what about circumcision? Some in Jerusalem thought it was essential. Antioch became the flash point for the controversy. "Men came down from Judea and were teaching the brothers, 'Unless you are circumcised . . . you cannot be saved'" (Acts 15:1). A council was called, and the matter was debated.

> *Some . . . rose up and said, "It is necessary to circumcise them and to order them to keep the law of Moses." . . . Peter stood up and said to them, "Brothers, you know that . . . God made a choice among you, that by my mouth the Gentiles should hear the word of the gospel and believe . . . why are you putting God to the test by placing a yoke on the neck of the disciples that neither our fathers nor we have been able to bear? But we believe that we will be saved through the grace of the Lord Jesus, just as they will." And all the assembly fell silent. (Acts 15:5-12)*

Nobody saw to the bottom of the issue more clearly than the apostle Paul. The very meaning of the suffering and death of Christ was at stake. Was faith in Christ enough to put us right with God? Or was circumcision necessary too? The answer was clear. If Paul preached circumcision, "the offense of the cross has been removed" (Galatians 5:11). The cross means freedom from the enslavement of ritual. "For freedom Christ has set us free; stand firm therefore, and do not submit again to a yoke of slavery" (Galatians 5:1).

TO BRING US TO FAITH AND KEEP US FAITHFUL

This is my blood of the covenant, which is poured out for many.
MARK 14:24

I will make with them an everlasting covenant. . . .
And I will put the fear of me in their hearts,
that they may not turn from me.
JEREMIAH 32:40

The Bible speaks of an "old covenant" and a "new covenant." The term *covenant* refers to a solemn, binding agreement between two parties carrying obligations for both sides and enforced by an oath. In the Bible the covenants God makes with man are initiated by himself. He sets the terms. His obligations are determined by his own purposes.

The "old covenant" refers to the arrangement God established with Israel in the law of Moses. Its weakness was that it was not accompanied by spiritual transformation. Therefore it was not obeyed and did not bring life. It was written with letters on stone, not with the Spirit on the heart. The prophets promised a "new covenant" that would be different. It would be "not of the letter but of the Spirit. For the letter kills, but the Spirit gives life" (2 Corinthians 3:6).

The new covenant is radically more effective than the old. It is enacted on the foundation of Jesus' suffering and death. "He is the mediator of a new covenant" (Hebrews 9:15). Jesus said that his blood was the "blood of the covenant, which is poured out for many" (Mark 14:24). This means that the blood of Jesus purchased the power and the promises of the new covenant. It is supremely effective because Christ died to make it so.

What then are the terms of the covenant that he infallibly secured by his blood? The prophet Jeremiah describes some of them: "I will make a new covenant . . . this is the covenant that I will make . . . I will put my law within them, and I will write it on their hearts. . . . For I will forgive their iniquity, and I will remember their sin no more" (Jeremiah 31:31-34). The suffering and death of Christ guarantees the inner change of his people (the law written on their hearts) and the forgiveness of their sins.

To guarantee that this covenant will not fail, Christ takes the initiative to create the faith and secure the faithfulness of his people. He brings a new-covenant people into being by writing the law not just on stone, but on the heart. In contrast with the "letter" on stone, he says "the Spirit gives life" (2 Corinthians 3:6). "When we were dead in our trespasses, [God] made us alive together with Christ" (Ephesians 2:5). This is the spiritual life that enables us to see and believe in the glory of Christ. This miracle creates the new-covenant people. It is sure and certain because Christ bought it with his own blood.

And the miracle is not only the creation of our faith, but the securing of our faithfulness. "I will make with them an everlasting covenant. . . . I will put the fear of me in their hearts, that they may not turn from me" (Jeremiah 32:40). When Christ died, he secured for his people not only new hearts but new security. He will not let them turn from him. He will keep them. They will persevere. The blood of the covenant guarantees it.

TO MAKE US HOLY, BLAMELESS, AND PERFECT

For by a single offering he has perfected for all time
those who are being sanctified.

Hebrews 10:14

He has now reconciled [you] in his body of flesh by his death,
in order to present you holy and blameless and
above reproach before him.

Colossians 1:22

Cleanse out the old leaven that you may be a new lump,
as you really are unleavened.
For Christ, our Passover lamb,
has been sacrificed.

1 Corinthians 5:7

One of the greatest heartaches in the Christian life is the slowness of our change. We hear the summons of God to love him with all our heart and soul and mind and strength (Mark 12:30). But do we ever rise to that totality of affection and devotion? We cry out regularly with the apostle Paul, "Wretched man that I am! Who will deliver me from this body of death?" (Romans 7:24). We groan even as we take fresh resolves: "Not that I have already obtained this or am already perfect, but I press on to make it my own, because Christ Jesus has made me his own" (Philippians 3:12).

That very statement is the key to endurance and joy. "Christ Jesus has made me his own." All my reaching and yearning and striving is not to belong to Christ (which has already happened), but to complete what is lacking in my likeness to him.

One of the greatest sources of joy and endurance for the Christian is knowing that in the imperfection of our progress we have already been perfected—and that this is owing to the suffering and death of Christ. "For by a single offering [namely, himself!] he has perfected for all time those who are being sanctified" (Hebrews 10:14). This is amazing! In the same sentence he says we are "being sanctified" and we are already "perfected."

Being sanctified means that we are imperfect and in process. We are becoming holy—but are not yet fully holy. And it is precisely these—and only these—who are already perfected. The joyful encouragement here is that the evidence of our perfection before God is not our experienced perfection, but our experienced progress. The good news is that being on the way is proof that we have arrived.

The Bible pictures this again in the old language of dough and leaven (yeast). In the picture, leaven is evil. We are the lump of dough. It says, "Cleanse out the old leaven that you may be a new lump, as you really are unleavened. For Christ, our Passover lamb, has been sacrificed" (1 Corinthians 5:7). Christians are "unleavened." There is no leaven—no evil. We are perfected. For this reason we are to "cleanse out the old leaven." We have been made unleavened in Christ. So we should now become unleavened in practice. In other words, we should become what we are.

The basis of all this? "For Christ, our Passover lamb, has been sacrificed." The suffering of Christ secures our perfection so firmly that it is already now a reality. Therefore, we fight against our sin not simply to *become* perfect, but because we *are*. The death of Jesus is the key to battling our imperfections on the firm foundation of our perfection.

TO GIVE US A CLEAR CONSCIENCE

How much more will the blood of Christ,
who through the eternal Spirit offered himself
without blemish to God, purify our conscience from
dead works to serve the living God.

Hebrews 9:14

Some things never change. The problem of a dirty conscience is as old as Adam and Eve. As soon as they sinned, their conscience was defiled. Their sense of guilt was ruinous. It ruined their relationship with God—they hid from him. It ruined their relation to each other—they blamed. It ruined their peace with themselves—for the first time they saw themselves and felt shame.

All through the Old Testament, conscience was an issue. But the animal sacrifices themselves could not cleanse the conscience. "Gifts and sacrifices are offered that cannot perfect the conscience of the worshiper, but deal only with food and drink and various washings, regulations for the body imposed until the time of reformation" (Hebrews 9:9-10). As a foreshadowing of Christ, God counted the blood of the animals as sufficient for cleansing the flesh—the ceremonial uncleanness, but not the conscience.

No animal blood could cleanse the conscience. They knew it (see Isaiah 53 and Psalm 51). And we know it. So a new high priest comes—Jesus the Son of God—with a better sacrifice: himself.

"How much more will the blood of Christ, who through the eternal Spirit offered himself without blemish to God, purify our conscience from dead works to serve the living God" (Hebrews 9:14). The animal sacrifices foreshadowed the final sacrifice of God's Son, and the death of the Son reaches back to cover all the sins of God's people in the old time period, and forward to cover all the sins of God's people in the new time period.

So here we are in the modern age—the age of science, Internet, organ transplants, instant messaging, cell phones—and our problem is fundamentally the same as always: Our conscience condemns us. We don't feel good enough to come to God. And no matter how distorted our consciences are, this much is true: We are not good enough to come to him.

We can cut ourselves, or throw our children in the sacred river, or give a million dollars to the United Way, or serve in a soup kitchen on Thanksgiving, or perform a hundred forms of penance and self-injury, and the result will be the same: The stain remains, and death terrifies. We know that our conscience is defiled—not with external things like touching a corpse or eating a piece of pork. Jesus said it is what comes out of a person that defiles, not what goes in (Mark 7:15-23). We are defiled by pride and self-pity and bitterness and lust and envy and jealousy and covetousness and apathy and fear—and the actions they breed. These are all "dead works." They have no spiritual life in them. They don't come from new life; they come from death, and they lead to death. That is why they make us feel hopeless in our consciences.

The only answer in these modern times, as in all other times, is the blood of Christ. When our conscience rises up and condemns us, where will we turn? We turn to Christ. We turn to the suffering and death of Christ—the blood of Christ. This is the only cleansing agent in the universe that can give the conscience relief in life and peace in death.

To Obtain for Us All Things That Are Good for Us

He who did not spare his own Son but gave him up for us all,
how will he not also with him graciously give us all things?

ROMANS 8:32

I love the logic of this verse. Not because I love logic, but because I love having my real needs met. The two halves of Romans 8:32 have a stupendously important logical connection. We may not see it, since the second half is a question: "How will he not also with him give us all things?" But if we change the question into the statement that it implies, we will see it. "He who did not spare his own Son but gave him up for us all, *will therefore surely* also with him graciously give us all things."

In other words, the connection between the two halves is meant to make the second half absolutely certain. If God did the hardest thing of all—namely, give up his own Son to suffering and death—then it is certain that he will do the comparatively easy thing, namely, give us all things with him. God's total commitment to give us all things is more sure than the sacrifice of his Son. He gave his Son "for us all." That done, could he stop being for us? It would be unthinkable.

But what does "give us all things" mean? Not an easy life of comfort. Not even safety from our enemies. We know this from what the Bible says four verses later: "For your sake we are being killed all the day long; we are regarded as sheep to be slaughtered" (Romans 8:36). Many Christians, even today, suffer this kind of persecution. When the Bible asks, "Shall tribulation, or distress, or persecution, or famine, or nakedness, or danger, or sword" separate us from the love of Christ (Romans 8:35), the answer is no. Not because these things don't happen to Christians, but because "in all these things we are more than conquerors through him who loved us" (Romans 8:37).

What then does it mean that because of Christ's death for us God will certainly with him graciously give us "all things"? It means that he will give us all things that are good for us. All things that we really need in order to be conformed to the image of his Son (Romans 8:29). All things we need in order to attain everlasting joy.

It's the same as the other biblical promise: "My God will supply *every need* of yours according to his riches in glory in Christ Jesus" (Philippians 4:19). This promise is clarified in the preceding words: "In any and every circumstance, I have learned the secret of facing plenty and *hunger*, abundance and *need*. I can do *all things* through him who strengthens me" (Philippians 4:12-13).

It says we can do "all things" through Christ. But notice "all things" includes "hungering" and "needing." God will meet every real need, including the ability to rejoice in suffering when many felt needs do not get met. God will meet every real need, including the need for grace to hunger when the felt need for food is not met. The suffering and death of Christ guarantee that God will give us all things that we need to do his will and to give him glory and to attain everlasting joy.

To Heal Us from Moral and Physical Sickness

Upon him was the chastisement that brought us peace,
and with his stripes we are healed.

Isaiah 53:5

[He] healed all who were sick.
This was to fulfill what was spoken by the prophet Isaiah:
"He took our illnesses and bore our diseases."

Matthew 8:16-17

Christ suffered and died so that disease would one day be utterly destroyed. Disease and death were not part of God's original way with the world. They came in with sin as part of God's judgment on creation. The Bible says, "The creation was subjected to futility, not willingly, but because of him who subjected it, in hope" (Romans 8:20). God subjected the world to the futility of physical pain to show the horror of moral evil.

This futility included death. "Sin came into the world through one man, and death through sin" (Romans 5:12). It included all the groaning of disease. And Christians are not excluded: "Not only the creation, but we ourselves, who have the firstfruits of the Spirit [that is, those who trust Christ], groan inwardly as we wait eagerly for adoption as sons, the redemption of our bodies" (Romans 8:23).

But all this misery of disease is temporary. We look forward to a time when bodily pain will be no more. The subjection of creation to futility was not permanent. From the very beginning of his judgment, the Bible says God aimed at hope. His final purpose was this: "that the creation itself will be set free from its bondage to decay and obtain the freedom of the glory of the children of God" (Romans 8:21).

When Christ came into the world, he was on a mission to accomplish this global redemption. He signaled his purposes by healing many people during his lifetime. There were occasions when the crowds gathered and he "healed all who were sick" (Matthew 8:16; Luke 6:19). This was a preview of what was coming at the end of history when "he will wipe away every tear from their eyes, and death shall be no more, neither shall there be mourning nor crying nor pain anymore" (Revelation 21:4).

The way Christ defeated death and disease was by taking them on himself and carrying them with him to the grave. God's judgment on the sin that brought disease was endured by Jesus when he suffered and died. The prophet Isaiah explained the death of Christ with these words: "He was wounded for our transgressions; he was crushed for our iniquities; upon him was the chastisement that brought us peace, and *with his stripes we are healed*" (Isaiah 53:5). The horrible blows to the back of Jesus bought a world without disease.

One day all disease will be banished from God's redeemed creation. There will be a new earth. We will have new bodies. Death will be swallowed up by everlasting life (1 Corinthians 15:54; 2 Corinthians 5:4). "The wolf and the lamb shall graze together; the lion shall eat straw like the ox" (Isaiah 65:25). And all who love Christ will sing songs of thanks to the Lamb who was slain to redeem us from sin and death and disease.

To Give Eternal Life to All Who Believe on Him

For God so loved the world, that he gave his only Son,
that whoever believes in him should not perish but have eternal life.
John 3:16

In our happiest times we do not want to die. The wish for death rises only when our suffering seems unbearable. What we really want in those times is not death, but relief. We would love for the good times to come again. We would like the pain to go away. We would like to have our loved one back from the grave. We want life and happiness.

We are kidding ourselves when we romanticize death as the climax of a life well lived. It is an enemy. It cuts us off from all the wonderful pleasures of this world. We call death sweet names only as the lesser of evils. The executioner that delivers the *coup de grace* in our suffering is not the fulfillment of longing, but the end of hope. The longing of the human heart is to live and to be happy.

God made us that way. "He has put eternity into man's heart" (Ecclesiastes 3:11). We are created in God's image, and God loves life and lives forever. We were made to live forever. And we will. The opposite of eternal life is not annihilation. It is hell. Jesus spoke of it more than anybody, and he made plain that rejecting the eternal life he offered would result not in obliteration, but in the misery of God's wrath: "Whoever believes in the Son has eternal life; whoever does not obey the Son shall not see life, but the wrath of God remains on him" (John 3:36).

And it remains forever. Jesus said, "These will go away into eternal punishment, but the righteous into eternal life" (Matthew 25:46). This is an unspeakable reality that shows the infinite evil of treating God with indifference or contempt. So Jesus warns, "If your eye causes you to sin, tear it out. It is better for you to enter the kingdom of God with one eye than with two eyes to be thrown into hell, 'where their worm does not die and the fire is not quenched'" (Mark 9:47-48).

So eternal life is not merely the extension of this life with its mix of pain and pleasure. As hell is the worst outcome of this life, so "eternal life" is the best. It is supreme and ever-increasing happiness where all sin and all sadness will be gone. All that is evil and harmful in this fallen creation will be removed. All that is good—all that will bring true and lasting happiness—will be preserved and purified and intensified.

We will be changed so that we are capable of dimensions of happiness that were inconceivable to us in this life. "What no eye has seen, nor ear heard, nor the heart of man imagined . . . God has prepared for those who love him" (1 Corinthians 2:9). It is true every moment of life, now and always: For those who trust Christ the best is yet to come. We will see the all-satisfying glory of God. "This is eternal life, that they know you the only true God, and Jesus Christ whom you have sent" (John 17:3). For this Christ suffered and died. Why would we not embrace him as our treasure, and live?

TO DELIVER US FROM THE PRESENT EVIL AGE

[He] gave himself for our sins to deliver us from the present evil age,
according to the will of our God and Father.

GALATIANS 1:4

Until we die, or until Christ returns to establish his kingdom, we live in "the present evil age." Therefore, when the Bible says that Christ gave himself "to deliver us from the present evil age," it does not mean that he will take us out of the world, but that he will deliver us from the power of the evil in it. Jesus prayed for us like this: "I do not ask that you take them out of the world, but that you keep them from the evil one" (John 17:15).

The reason Jesus prays for deliverance from "the evil one" is that "this present evil age" is the age when Satan is given freedom to deceive and destroy. The Bible says, "The whole world lies in the power of the evil one" (1 John 5:19). This "evil one" is called "the god of this world," and his main aim is to blind people to truth. "The god of this world has blinded the minds of the unbelievers, to keep them from seeing the light of the gospel of the glory of Christ" (2 Corinthians 4:4).

Until we waken to our darkened spiritual condition, we live in sync with "the present evil age" and the ruler of it. "You once walked, following the course of this world, following the prince of the power of the air, the spirit that is now at work in the sons of disobedience" (Ephesians 2:2). Without knowing it, we were lackeys of the devil. What felt like freedom was bondage. The Bible speaks straight to twenty-first-century fads, fun, and addictions when it says, "They promise them freedom, but they themselves are slaves of corruption. For whatever overcomes a person, to that he is enslaved" (2 Peter 2:19).

The resounding cry of freedom in the Bible is, "Do not be conformed to this world, but be transformed by the renewal of your mind" (Romans 12:2). In other words, be free! Don't be duped by the gurus of the age. They are here today and gone tomorrow. One enslaving fad follows another. Thirty years from now today's tattoos will not be marks of freedom, but indelible reminders of conformity.

The wisdom of this age is folly in view of eternity. "Let no one deceive himself. If anyone among you thinks that he is wise in this age, let him become a fool that he may become wise. For the wisdom of this world is folly with God" (1 Corinthians 3:18-19). "The word of the cross is folly to those who are perishing" (1 Corinthians 1:18). What then is the wisdom of God in this age? It is the great liberating death of Jesus Christ. The early followers of Jesus said, "We preach Christ crucified . . . the power of God and the wisdom of God" (1 Corinthians 1:23-24).

When Christ went to the cross, he set millions of captives free. He unmasked the devil's fraud and broke his power. That's what he meant on the eve of his crucifixion when he said, "Now will the ruler of this world be cast out" (John 12:31). Don't follow a defeated foe. Follow Christ. It is costly. You will be an exile in this age. But you will be free.

To Reconcile Us to God

*For if while we were enemies we were reconciled to God
by the death of his Son, much more, now that
we are reconciled, shall we be saved by his life.*

Romans 5:10

The reconciliation that needs to happen between sinful man and God goes both ways. Our attitude toward God must be changed from defiance to faith. And God's attitude to us must be changed from wrath to mercy. But the two are not the same. I need God's help to change; but God does not need mine. My change will have to come from outside of me, but God's change originates in his own nature. Which means that overall, it is not a change in God at all. It is God's own planned action to stop being against me and start being for me.

The all-important words are "while we were enemies." This is when "we were reconciled to God by the death of his Son" (Romans 5:10). While we were *enemies*. In other words, the first "change" was God's, not ours. We were still enemies. Not that we were consciously on the warpath. Most people don't feel conscious hostility to God. The hostility is manifest more subtly with a quiet insubordination and indifference. The Bible describes it like this: "The mind that is set on the flesh is hostile to God, for it does not submit to God's law; indeed, it cannot" (Romans 8:7).

While we were still like that, God put Christ forward to bear our wrath-kindling sins and make it possible for him to treat us with mercy alone. God's first act in reconciling us to himself was to remove the obstacle that made him irreconcilable, namely, the God-belittling guilt of our sin. "In Christ God was reconciling the world to himself, not counting their trespasses against them" (2 Corinthians 5:19).

When the ambassadors of Christ take this message to the world, they say, "We implore you on behalf of Christ, be reconciled to God" (2 Corinthians 5:20). Do they only mean: Change your attitude to God? No, they also mean: Receive the prior work of God in Christ to reconcile himself to you.

Consider this analogy of reconciliation among men. Jesus said, "If you are offering your gift at the altar and there remember that your brother has something against you, leave your gift there before the altar and go. First be reconciled to your brother, and then come and offer your gift" (Matthew 5:23-24). When he says, "Be reconciled to your brother," notice that it is the brother who must remove his judgment. The brother is the one who "has something against you," just as God has something against us. "Be reconciled to your brother" means do what you must so that your brother's judgment against you will be removed.

But when we hear the gospel of Christ, we find that God has already done that: He took the steps we could not take to remove his own judgment. He sent Christ to suffer in our place. The decisive reconciliation happened "while we were enemies." Reconciliation from our side is simply to receive what God has already done, the way we receive an infinitely valuable gift.

To Bring Us to God

*Christ also suffered once for sins, the righteous
for the unrighteous, that he might bring us to God.*

1 Peter 3:18

*But now in Christ Jesus you who once were far off
have been brought near by the blood of Christ.*

Ephesians 2:13

When all is said and done, God is the gospel. Gospel means "good news." Christianity is not first theology, but news. It is like prisoners of war hearing by hidden radio that the allies have landed and rescue is only a matter of time. The guards wonder why all the rejoicing.

But what is the ultimate good in the good news? It all ends in one thing: God himself. All the words of the gospel lead to him, or they are not gospel. For example, salvation is not good news if it only saves from hell and not for God. Forgiveness is not good news if it only gives relief from guilt and doesn't open the way to God. Justification is not good news if it only makes us legally acceptable to God but doesn't bring fellowship with God. Redemption is not good news if it only liberates us from bondage but doesn't bring us to God. Adoption is not good news if it only puts us in the Father's family but not in his arms.

This is crucial. Many people seem to embrace the good news without embracing God. There is no sure evidence that we have a new heart just because we want to escape hell. That's a perfectly natural desire, not a supernatural one. It doesn't take a new heart to want the psychological relief of forgiveness, or the removal of God's wrath, or the inheritance of God's world. All these things are understandable without any spiritual change. You don't need to be born again to want these things. The devils want them.

It is not wrong to want them. Indeed it is folly not to. But the evidence that we have been changed is that we want these things because they bring us to the enjoyment of God. This is the greatest thing Christ died for. "Christ also suffered once for sins, the righteous for the unrighteous, *that he might bring us to God*" (1 Peter 3:18).

Why is this the essence of the good news? Because we were made to experience full and lasting happiness from seeing and savoring the glory of God. If our best joy comes from something less, we are idolaters and God is dishonored. He created us in such a way that his glory is displayed through our joy in it. The gospel of Christ is the good news that at the cost of his Son's life, God has done everything necessary to enthrall us with what will make us eternally and ever-increasingly happy, namely, himself.

Long before Christ came, God revealed himself as the source of full and lasting pleasure. "You make known to me the path of life; in your presence there is fullness of joy; at your right hand are pleasures forevermore" (Psalm 16:11). Then he sent Christ to suffer "that he might bring us to God." This means he sent Christ to bring us to the deepest, longest joy a human can have. Hear then the invitation: Turn from "the fleeting pleasures of sin" (Hebrews 11:25) and come to "pleasures forevermore." Come to Christ.

SO THAT WE MIGHT BELONG TO HIM

You also have died to the law through the body of Christ,
so that you may belong to another,
to him who has been raised from the dead.

Romans 7:4

You are not your own,
for you were bought with a price.

1 Corinthians 6:19-20

Care for the church of God,
which he obtained with his own blood.

Acts 20:28

The ultimate question is not *who* you are but *whose* you are. Of course, many people think they are nobody's slave. They dream of total independence. Like a jellyfish carried by the tides feels free because it isn't fastened down with the bondage of barnacles.

But Jesus had a word for people who thought that way. He said, "You will know the truth, and the truth will set you free." But they responded, "We . . . have never been enslaved to anyone. How is it that you say, 'You will become free'?" So Jesus answered, "Truly, truly, I say to you, everyone who commits sin is a slave to sin" (John 8:32-34).

The Bible gives no reality to fallen humans who are ultimately self-determining. There is no autonomy in the fallen world. We are governed by sin or governed by God. "You are slaves of the one whom you obey. . . . When you were slaves of sin, you were free in regard to righteousness. . . . But now . . . you have been set free from sin and have become slaves of God" (Romans 6:16, 20, 22).

Most of the time we are free to do what we want. But we are not free to want what we ought. For that we need a new power based on a divine purchase. The *power* is God's. Which is why the Bible says, "Thanks be to *God*, that you who were once slaves of sin have become obedient from the heart" (Romans 6:17). God is the one who may "grant them repentance leading to a knowledge of the truth, and they may escape from the snare of the devil, after being captured by him to do his will" (2 Timothy 2:25-26).

And the *purchase* that unleashes this power is the death of Christ. "You are not your own, for you were bought with a price" (1 Corinthians 6:19-20). And what price did Christ pay for those who trust him? "He obtained [them] with his own blood" (Acts 20:28).

Now we are free indeed. Not to be autonomous, but to want what is good. A whole new way of life opens to us when the death of Christ becomes the death of our old self. Relationship with the living Christ replaces rules. And the freedom of fruit-bearing replaces the bondage of law. "You also have died to the law through the body of Christ, *so that you may belong to another*, to him who has been raised from the dead, in order that we may bear fruit for God" (Romans 7:4).

Christ suffered and died that we might be set free from law and sin and belong to him. Here is where obedience ceases to be a burden and becomes the freedom of fruit-bearing. Remember, you are not your own. Whose will you be? If Christ's, then come and belong.

To Give Us Confident Access to the Holiest Place

*We have confidence to enter the holy places
by the blood of Jesus.*
Hebrews 10:19

O ne of the great mysteries in the Old Testament was the meaning of the worship tent used by Israel called the "tabernacle." The mystery was hinted at but not clear. When the people of Israel came out of Egypt and arrived at Mount Sinai, God gave detailed instructions to Moses about how to build this mobile tent of worship with all its parts and furnishings. The mysterious thing about it was this command: "See that you make them after the pattern for them, which is being shown you on the mountain" (Exodus 25:40).

When Christ came into the world 1,400 years later, it was more fully revealed that this "pattern" for the old tabernacle was a "copy" or a "shadow" of realities in heaven. The tabernacle was an earthly figure of a heavenly reality. So in the New Testament we read this: "[The priests] serve a copy and shadow of the heavenly things. For when Moses was about to erect the tent, he was instructed by God, saying, 'See that you make everything according to the pattern that was shown you on the mountain'" (Hebrews 8:5).

So all the worship practices of Israel in the Old Testament point toward something more real. Just as there were holy rooms in the tabernacle, where the priest repeatedly took the blood of the animal sacrifices and met with God, so there are infinitely superior "holy places," as it were, in heaven, where Christ entered with his own blood, not repeatedly, but once for all.

> When Christ appeared as a high priest . . . through the greater and more perfect tent (not made with hands, that is, not of this creation) he entered once for all into the holy places, not by means of the blood of goats and calves but by means of his own blood, thus securing an eternal redemption. (Hebrews 9:11-12)

The implication of this for us is that the way is now opened for us to go with Christ into all the holiest places of God's presence. Formerly only the Jewish priests could go into the "copy" and "shadow" of these places. Only the high priest could go once a year into the most holy place where the glory of God appeared (Hebrews 9:7). There was a forbidding curtain protecting the place of glory. The Bible tells us that when Christ breathed his last on the cross, "the curtain of the temple was torn in two, from top to bottom. And the earth shook, and the rocks were split" (Matthew 27:51).

What did that mean? The interpretation is given in these words: "We have confidence to enter the holy places by the blood of Jesus, by the new and living way that he opened for us through the curtain, that is, through his flesh" (Hebrews 10:19-20). Without Christ the holiness of God had to be protected from us. He would have been dishonored, and we would have been consumed because of our sin. But now, because of Christ, we may come near and feast our hearts on the fullness of the flaming beauty of God's holiness. He will not be dishonored . We will not be consumed. Because of the all-protecting Christ, God will be honored, and we will stand in everlasting awe. Therefore, do not fear to come. But come through Christ.

TO BECOME FOR US THE PLACE WHERE WE MEET GOD

*Jesus answered them, "Destroy this temple, and in three days
I will raise it up." The Jews then said,
"It has taken forty-six years to build this temple,
and will you raise it up in three days?"
But he was speaking about the temple of his body.*

John 2:19-21

Kill me, and I will become the global meeting place with God."
That's the way I would paraphrase John 2:19-21. They
thought Jesus was referring to the temple in Jerusalem: "Destroy
this temple, and in three days I will raise it up." But he was referring to his body.

Why did Jesus draw the connection between the Jewish temple and his own body? Because he came to take the place of the
temple as the meeting place with God. With the coming of the Son
of God in human flesh, ritual and worship would undergo profound change. Christ himself would become the final Passover
lamb, the final priest, the final temple. They would all pass away,
and he would remain.

What remained would be infinitely better. Referring to himself,
Jesus said, "I tell you, something greater than the temple is here"
(Matthew 12:6). The temple became the dwelling of God at rare
times when the glory of God filled the holy place. But of Christ

the Bible says, "In him the whole fullness of deity dwells bodily" (Colossians 2:9). The presence of God does not come and go on Jesus. He is God. Where we meet him, we meet God.

God met the people in the temple through many imperfect human mediators. But now it is said of Christ, "There is one mediator between God and men, the man Christ Jesus" (1 Timothy 2:5). If we would meet God in worship, there is only one place we must go, to Jesus Christ. Christianity has no geographical center like Islam and Judaism.

Once when Jesus confronted a woman with her adultery, she changed the subject and said, "Our fathers worshiped on this mountain, but you say that in Jerusalem is the place where people ought to worship." Jesus followed her on the detour: "Woman, . . . the hour is coming when neither on this mountain nor in Jerusalem will you worship the Father." Geography is not the issue. What is? Jesus continued, "The hour is coming, and is now here, when the true worshipers will worship the Father in spirit and truth" (John 4:20-23).

Jesus changes the categories entirely. Not in this *mountain* or in that *city*, but in *spirit* and in *truth*. He came into the world to explode geographical limitation. There is no temple now. Jerusalem is not the center. Christ is. Do we want to see God? Jesus says, "Whoever has seen me has seen the Father" (John 14:9). Do we want to receive God? Jesus says, "Whoever receives me receives him who sent me" (Matthew 10:40). Do we want to have the presence of God in worship? The Bible says, "Whoever confesses the Son has the Father also" (1 John 2:23). Do we want to honor the Father? Jesus says, "Whoever does not honor the Son does not honor the Father who sent him" (John 5:23).

When Christ died and rose again, the old temple was replaced by the globally accessible Christ. You may come to him without moving a muscle. He is as close as faith.

To Bring the Old Testament Priesthood to an End and Become the Eternal High Priest

The former priests . . . were prevented by death from continuing in office, but he holds his priesthood permanently, because he continues forever. Consequently, he is able to save to the uttermost those who draw near to God through him, since he always lives to make intercession for them. . . . He has no need, like those high priests, to offer sacrifices daily, first for his own sins and then for those of the people, since he did this once for all when he offered up himself.

Hebrews 7:23-27

For Christ has entered . . . into heaven itself, now to appear in the presence of God on our behalf. Nor was it to offer himself repeatedly, as the high priest enters the holy places every year with blood not his own, for then he would have had to suffer repeatedly since the foundation of the world. But as it is, he has appeared once for all at the end of the ages to put away sin by the sacrifice of himself.

Hebrews 9:24-26

Every priest stands daily at his service,
offering repeatedly the same sacrifices,
which can never take away sins.
But when Christ had offered for all
time a single sacrifice for sins,
he sat down at the right hand of God.

Hebrews 10:11-12

One of the greatest phrases of Christian truth is "once for all." It comes from one Greek word (*ephapax*) and means "once for all time." It means that something happened that was decisive. The act accomplished so much that it need never be repeated. Any effort to repeat it would discredit the achievement that happened "once for all."

It was a gloomy reality year after year that the priests in Israel had to offer animal sacrifices for their own sins and the sins of the people. I don't mean there was no forgiveness. God appointed these sacrifices for the relief of his people. They sinned and needed a substitute to bear their punishment. It was mercy that God accepted the ministry of sinful priests and substitute animals.

But there was a dark side to it. It had to be done over and over. The Bible says, "In these sacrifices there is a reminder of sin every year" (Hebrews 10:3). The people knew that when they laid their hands on the head of a bull to transfer their sins to the animal, it would all have to be done again. No animal could suffice to suffer for human sins. Sinful priests had to sacrifice for their own sins. Mortal priests had to be replaced. Bulls and goats had no moral life and could not bear the guilt of man. "It is impossible for the blood of bulls and goats to take away sins" (Hebrews 10:4).

But there was a silver lining around this cloud of priestly insufficiency. If God honored these inadequate things, it must mean that one day he would send a servant qualified to complete what these priests could not perform—to put away sin once for all.

That's who Jesus Christ is. He became the final Priest and the final Sacrifice. *Sinless*, he did not offer sacrifices for himself. *Immortal*, he never has to be replaced. *Human*, he could bear human sins. Therefore he did not offer sacrifices for himself; he offered himself as the final sacrifice. There will never be the need for another. There is one mediator between us and God. One priest. We need no other. Oh, how happy are those who draw near to God through Christ alone.

To Become a Sympathetic and Helpful Priest

For we do not have a high priest who is unable to sympathize with our weaknesses, but one who in every respect has been tempted as we are, yet without sin. Let us then with confidence draw near to the throne of grace, that we may receive mercy and find grace to help in time of need.

Hebrews 4:15-16

Christ became our Priest by the sacrifice of himself on the cross (Hebrews 9:26). He is our go-between with God. His obedience and suffering were so perfect that God will not turn him away. Therefore, if we go to God through him, God will not turn us away either.

But it gets even better. On the way to the cross for thirty years, Christ was tempted like every human is tempted. True, he never sinned. But wise people have pointed out that this means his temptations were stronger than ours, not weaker. If a person gives in to temptation, it never reaches its fullest and longest assault. We capitulate while the pressure is still building. But Jesus never did. So he endured the full pressure to the end and never caved. He knows what it is to be tempted with fullest force.

A lifetime of temptation climaxing in spectacular abuse and abandonment gave Jesus an unparalleled ability to sympathize with tempted and suffering people. No one has ever suffered more.

No one has ever endured more abuse. And no one ever deserved it less or had a greater right to fight back. But the apostle Peter said, "He committed no sin, neither was deceit found in his mouth. When he was reviled, he did not revile in return; when he suffered, he did not threaten, but continued entrusting himself to him who judges justly" (1 Peter 2:22-23).

Therefore, the Bible says he is able "to sympathize with our weaknesses" (Hebrews 4:15). This is amazing. The risen Son of God in heaven at God's right hand with all authority over the universe feels what we feel when we come to him in sorrow or pain— or cornered with the promises of sinful pleasure.

What difference does this make? The Bible answers by making a connection between Jesus' sympathy and our confidence in prayer. It says that since he is able to "sympathize with our weaknesses . . . [*therefore* we should] with confidence draw near to the throne of grace, that we may receive mercy and find grace to help in time of need" (Hebrews 4:15-16).

Evidently the thought goes like this: We are likely to feel unwelcome in the presence of God if we come with struggles. We feel God's purity and perfection so keenly that everything about us seems unsuitable in his presence. But then we remember that Jesus is "sympathetic." He feels *with* us, not *against* us. This awareness of Christ's sympathy makes us bold to come. He knows our cry. He tasted our struggle. He bids us come with confidence when we feel our need. So let's remember the old song of John Newton:

> *Thou art coming to a King.*
> *Large petitions with thee bring;*
> *For his grace and pow'r are such*
> *None can ever ask too much.*[4]

To Free Us from the Futility of Our Ancestry

You were ransomed from the futile ways inherited from
your forefathers, not with perishable things such as silver or gold,
but with the precious blood of Christ,
like that of a lamb without blemish or spot.

1 Peter 1:18-19

Secular people in the West, and more primitive people in animistic tribes, have this in common: They believe in the power of ancestral bondage. They call it by different names. Animistic people may speak in terms of ancestral spirits and the transmission of curses. Secular people may speak of genetic influence or the wounding of abusive, codependent, emotionally distant parents. In both cases there is a sense of fatalism that we are bound to live with the curse or the wounds from our ancestry. The future seems futile and void of happiness.

When the Bible says, "You were ransomed from the futile ways inherited from your forefathers," it is referring to an empty, meaningless, unprofitable way of living that ends with destruction. It says that these "futile ways" are connected with our ancestors. It doesn't say how. The crucial thing is to notice how we are freed from the bondage of this futility. The power of the liberator defines the extent of the liberation.

The liberation from ancestral bondage happens "not with perishable things such as silver or gold." Silver and gold represent the most valuable things that could be paid for our ransom. But we all know they are useless. The richest people are often the most enslaved to the futility. A wealthy tribal chief may be tormented by the fear of an ancestral hex on his life. A secular president of a successful company may be driven by unconscious forces from his background that ruin his marriage and children.

Silver and gold are powerless to help. The suffering and death of Jesus provide what is needed: not gold or silver but "the precious blood of Christ, like that of a lamb without blemish or spot." When Christ died, God had a view to the relationship between us and our ancestors. He meant to set us free from the futility we inherited from them. That is one of the great reasons Christ died.

No hex can hold against you, if your sins are all forgiven, and you are clothed with the righteousness of Christ, and you are ransomed and loved by the Creator of the universe. The suffering and death of Jesus is the final reason why the Bible says of God's people, "There is no enchantment against Jacob, no divination against Israel" (Numbers 23:23). When Jesus died, all the blessings of heaven were purchased for those who trust him. And when God blesses, none can curse.

Nor is any wound that was inflicted by a parent beyond the healing of Jesus. The healing ransom is called "the precious blood of Christ." The word "precious" conveys infinite value. Therefore the ransom is infinitely liberating. No bondage can stand against it. Therefore, let us turn from silver and gold and embrace the gift of God.

TO FREE US FROM THE SLAVERY OF SIN

*To him who loves us and has freed us from our sins by his blood
and made us a kingdom, priests to his God and Father,
to him be glory and dominion forever and ever.*

Revelation 1:5-6

*Jesus also suffered outside the gate
in order to sanctify the people through his own blood.*

Hebrews 13:12

Our sin ruins us in two ways. It makes us guilty before God, so that we are under his just condemnation; and it makes us ugly in our behavior, so that we disfigure the image of God we were meant to display. It damns us with guilt, and it enslaves us to lovelessness.

The blood of Jesus frees us from both miseries. It satisfies God's righteousness so that our sins can be justly forgiven. And it defeats the power of sin to make us slaves to lovelessness. We have seen how Christ absorbs the wrath of God and takes away our guilt. But now how does the blood of Christ liberate us from the slavery of sin?

The answer is not that he is a powerful example to us and inspires us to free ourselves from selfishness. Oh, yes, Jesus is an example to us. And a very powerful one. He clearly meant for us to imitate him: "A new commandment I give to you, that you love one another: just as I have loved you, you also are to love one another" (John 13:34). But the call to imitation is not the power of liberation. There is something deeper.

Sin is such a powerful influence in our lives that we must be liberated by God's power, not by our willpower. But since we are sinners we must ask, Is the power of God directed toward our liberation or our condemnation? That's where the suffering of Christ comes in. When Christ died to remove our condemnation, he opened, as it were, the valve of heaven's mighty mercy to flow on behalf of our liberation from the power of sin.

In other words, rescue from the *guilt* of sin and the wrath of God had to precede rescue from the *power* of sin by the mercy of God. The crucial biblical words for saying this are: *Justification* precedes and secures *sanctification*. They are different. One is an instantaneous declaration (not guilty!); the other is an ongoing transformation.

Now, for those who are trusting Christ, the power of God is not in the service of his condemning wrath, but his liberating mercy. God gives us this power for change through the person of his Holy Spirit. That is why the beauty of "love, joy, peace, patience, kindness, goodness, faithfulness, gentleness, self-control" are called "the fruit of the Spirit" (Galatians 5:22-23). This is why the Bible can make the amazing promise: "Sin will have no dominion over you, since you are not under law but under grace" (Romans 6:14). Being "under grace" secures the omnipotent power of God to destroy our lovelessness (not all at once, but progressively). We are not passive in the defeat of our selfishness, but neither do we provide the decisive power. It is God's grace. Hence the great apostle Paul said, "I worked harder than any of them, though it was not I, but the grace of God that is with me" (1 Corinthians 15:10). May the God of all grace, by faith in Christ, free us from both the guilt and slavery of sin.

THAT WE MIGHT DIE TO SIN AND LIVE TO RIGHTEOUSNESS

He himself bore our sins in his body on the tree,
that we might die to sin and live to righteousness.

1 Peter 2:24

Strange as it may sound, Christ's dying in our place and for our sins means that *we* died. You would think that having a substitute die in your place would mean that you escape death. And, of course, we do escape death—the *eternal* death of endless misery and separation from God. Jesus said, "I give them eternal life, and they will *never perish*" (John 10:28). "Everyone who lives and believes in me *shall never die*" (John 11:26). The death of Jesus *does* indeed mean that "whoever believes in him should *not perish* but have eternal life" (John 3:16).

But there is another sense in which we die precisely because Christ died in our place and for our sins. "He himself bore our sins in his body on the tree, that we might die . . ." (1 Peter 2:24). He died that we might live; and he died that we might die. When Christ died, I, as a believer in Christ, died with him. The Bible is clear: "We have been united with him in a death like his" (Romans 6:5). "One has died for all, therefore all have died" (2 Corinthians 5:14).

Faith is the evidence of being united to Christ in this profound way. Believers "have been crucified with Christ" (Galatians 2:20).

We look back on his death and know that, in the mind of God, we were there. Our sins were on him, and the death we deserved was happening to us in him. Baptism signifies this death with Christ. "We were buried . . . with him *by baptism* into death" (Romans 6:4). The water is like a grave. Going under is a picture of death. Coming up is a picture of new life. And it is all a picture of what God is doing "through faith." "[You have] been buried with him in baptism, in which you were also raised with him *through faith* in the powerful working of God" (Colossians 2:12).

The fact that I died with Christ is linked directly to his dying for my sin. "He himself *bore our sins . . . that we might die*." This means that when I embrace Jesus as my Savior, I embrace my own death as a sinner. My sin brought Jesus to the grave and brought me there with him. Faith sees sin as murderous. It killed Jesus, and it killed me.

Therefore, becoming a Christian means death to sin. The old self that loved sin died with Jesus. Sin is like a prostitute that no longer looks beautiful. She is the murderer of my King and myself. Therefore, the believer is dead to sin, no longer dominated by her attractions. Sin, the prostitute who killed my friend, has no appeal. She has become an enemy.

My new life is now swayed by righteousness. "He himself bore our sins in his body on the tree, that we might . . . *live to righteousness*" (1 Peter 2:24). The beauty of Christ, who loved me and gave himself for me, is the desire of my soul. And his beauty is perfect righteousness. The command that I now love to obey is this (and I invite you to join me): "Present yourselves to God as those who have been brought from death to life, and your members to God as instruments for righteousness" (Romans 6:13).

So That We Would Die to the Law and Bear Fruit for God

You also have died to the law through the body of Christ,
so that you may belong to another, to him who has been raised
from the dead, in order that we may bear fruit for God.

ROMANS 7:4

When Christ died for us, we died with him. God looked on us who believe as united to Christ. His death for our sin was our death in him. (See the previous chapter.) But sin was not the only reality that killed Jesus and us. So did the law of God. When we break the law by sinning, the law sentences us to death. If there were no law, there would be no punishment. "For . . . where there is no law there is no transgression" (Romans 4:15). But "whatever the law says it speaks to those who are under the law, so that . . . the whole world may be held accountable to God" (Romans 3:19).

There was no escape from the curse of the law. It was just; we were guilty. There was only one way to be free: Someone must pay the penalty. That's why Jesus came: "Christ redeemed us from the curse of the law by becoming a curse for us" (Galatians 3:13).

Therefore, God's law cannot condemn us if we are in Christ. Its power to rule us is doubly broken. On the one hand, the law's demands have been fulfilled by Christ on our behalf. His perfect law-keeping is credited to our account (see chapter 11). On the other hand, the law's penalty has been paid by the blood of Christ.

This is why the Bible so clearly teaches that getting right with God is not based on law-keeping. "By works of the law no human being will be justified in his sight" (Romans 3:20). "A person is not justified by works of the law but through faith in Jesus Christ" (Galatians 2:16). There is no hope of getting right with God by law-keeping. The only hope is the blood and righteousness of Christ, which is ours by faith alone. "We hold that one is justified by faith apart from works of the law" (Romans 3:28).

How then do we please God, if we are dead to his law and it is no longer our master? Is not the law the expression of God's good and holy will (Romans 7:12)? The biblical answer is that instead of belonging to the law, which demands and condemns, we now belong to Christ who demands and gives. Formerly, righteousness was demanded from outside in letters written in stone. But now righteousness rises within us as a longing in our relationship with Christ. He is present and real. By his Spirit he helps us in our weakness. A living person has replaced a lethal list. "The letter kills, but the Spirit gives life" (2 Corinthians 3:6). (See chapter 14.)

This is why the Bible says that the new way of obedience is *fruit-bearing*, not law-keeping. "You . . . have died to the law through the body of Christ, so that you may belong to another, to him who has been raised from the dead, *in order that we may bear fruit for God*" (Romans 7:4). We have died to law-keeping so that we might live to fruit-bearing. Fruit grows naturally on a tree. If the tree is good, the fruit will be good. And the tree, in this case, is a living relationship of love to Jesus Christ. For this he died. Now he bids us come: "Trust me." Die to the law, that you might bear the fruit of love.

To Enable Us to Live for Christ and Not Ourselves

He died for all, that those who live might no longer live
for themselves but for him who for their sake died and was raised.
2 Corinthians 5:15

I t troubles a lot of people that Christ died to exalt Christ. Boiled down to its essence, 2 Corinthians 5:15 says Christ died for us that we might live for him. In other words, he died for us so that we make much of him. Bluntly, Christ died for Christ.

Now that is true. It's not a word trick. The very essence of sin is that we have failed to glorify God—which includes failing to glorify his Son (Romans 3:23). But Christ died to bear that sin and to free us from it. So he died to bear the dishonor that we had heaped on him by our sin. He died to turn this around. Christ died for the glory of Christ.

The reason this troubles people is that it sounds vain. It doesn't seem like a loving thing to do. So it seems to turn the suffering of Christ into the very opposite of what the Bible says it is, namely, the supreme act of love. But in fact it's both. Christ's dying for his own glory and his dying to show love are not only both *true*, they are both *the same*.

Christ is unique. No one else can act this way and call it love. Christ is the only human in the universe who is also God and therefore infinitely valuable. He is infinitely beautiful in all his moral perfections. He is infinitely wise and just and good and strong. "He is the radiance of the glory of God and the exact imprint of his nature" (Hebrews 1:3). To see him and know him is more satisfying than having all that earth can offer.

Those who knew him best spoke this way:

> *Whatever gain I had, I counted as loss for the sake of Christ. Indeed, I count everything as loss because of the surpassing worth of knowing Christ Jesus my Lord. For his sake I have suffered the loss of all things and count them as rubbish, in order that I may gain Christ. (Philippians 3:7-8)*

"Christ died that we might live for him" does not mean "that we might *help* him." "[God is not] served by human hands, as though he needed anything" (Acts 17:25). Neither is Christ: "The Son of Man came *not to be served* but to serve, and to give his life as a ransom for many" (Mark 10:45). What Christ died for is not that we might help him, but that we might see and savor him as infinitely valuable. He died to wean us from poisonous pleasures and enthrall us with the pleasures of his beauty. In this way we are loved, and he is honored. These are not competing aims. They are one.

Jesus said to his disciples that he had to go away so that he could send the Holy Spirit, the Helper (John 16:7). Then he told them what the Helper would do when he came: "He will glorify me" (John 16:14). Christ died and rose so that we would see and magnify him. This is the greatest help in the world. This is love. The most loving prayer Jesus ever prayed was this: "Father, I desire that they also, whom you have given me, may be with me where I am, to see my glory" (John 17:24). For this Christ died. This is love—suffering to give us everlasting enjoyment, namely himself.

To Make His Cross the Ground of All Our Boasting

Far be it from me to boast except in the cross of our Lord Jesus Christ, by which the world has been crucified to me, and I to the world.

Galatians 6:14

This seems over the top. Boast only in the cross! Really? Literally *only* in the cross? Even the Bible talks about other things to boast in. Boast in the glory of God (Romans 5:2). Boast in our tribulations (Romans 5:3). Boast in our weaknesses (2 Corinthians 12:9). Boast in the people of Christ (1 Thessalonians 2:19). What does "only" mean here?

It means that all other boasting should still be a boasting in the cross. If we boast in the hope of glory, that very boast should be a boast in the cross of Christ. If we boast in the people of Christ, that very boasting should be a boasting in the cross. Boasting only in the cross means only the cross enables every other legitimate boast, and every legitimate boast should therefore honor the cross.

Why? Because every good thing—indeed, even every bad thing that God turns for good—was obtained for us by the cross of Christ. Apart from faith in Christ, sinners get only judgment. Yes, there are many pleasant things that come to unbelievers.

But the Bible teaches that even these natural blessings of life will only increase the severity of God's judgment in the end, if they are not received with thanks on the basis of Christ's sufferings (Romans 2:4-5).

Therefore, everything that we enjoy, as people who trust Christ, is owing to his death. His suffering absorbed all the judgment that guilty sinners deserved and purchased all the good that forgiven sinners enjoy. Therefore all our boasting in these things should be a boasting in the cross of Christ. We are not as Christ-centered and cross-cherishing as we should be, because we do not ponder the truth that everything good, and everything bad that God turns for the good, was purchased by the sufferings of Christ.

And how do we become that radically cross-focused? We must awaken to the truth that when Christ died on the cross, we died (see chapter 31). When this happened to the apostle Paul, he said, "The world has been crucified to me, and I to the world" (Galatians 6:14). This is the key to Christ-centered boasting in the cross.

When you put your trust in Christ, the overpowering attraction of the world is broken. You are a corpse to the world, and the world is a corpse to you. Or to put it positively, you are a "new creation" (Galatians 6:15). The old you is dead. A new you is alive—the you of faith in Christ. And what marks this faith is that it treasures Christ above everything in the world. The power of the world to woo your love away has died.

Being dead to the world means that every legitimate pleasure in the world becomes a blood-bought evidence of Christ's love and an occasion of boasting in the cross. When our hearts run back along the beam of blessing to the source in the cross, then the worldliness of the blessing is dead, and Christ crucified is everything.

To Enable Us to Live by Faith in Him

I have been crucified with Christ. It is no longer I who live,
but Christ who lives in me. And the life I now live in the flesh
I live by faith in the Son of God, who loved me
and gave himself for me.

Galatians 2:20

There is an explicit paradox in this verse. "I have been crucified," but "I now live." But you might say, "That's not paradoxical, it's just sequential. First I died with Christ; then I was raised with him and now live." True. But what about these even more paradoxical words: "It is no longer I who live," yet "I now live"? Do I live or don't I?

Paradoxes are not contradictions. They just sound that way. What Paul means is that there was an "I" who died, and there is a different "I" who lives. That's what it means to become a Christian. An old self dies. A new self is "created" or "raised." "If anyone is in Christ, he is a new *creation*" (2 Corinthians 5:17). "When we were dead in our trespasses, [God] made us alive together with Christ . . . and *raised* us up with him" (Ephesians 2:5-6).

The aim of the death of Christ was to take our "old self" with him into the grave and put an end to it. "We know that our *old self* was crucified with him in order that the body of sin might be brought to nothing" (Romans 6:6). If we trust Christ, we are united to him, and God counts our old self as dying with Christ. The purpose was the raising of a new self.

So who is the new self? What's different about these two selves? Am I still me? The verse at the beginning of this chapter describes the new self in two ways: One way is almost unimaginable; the other is plain. First, it says that the new self is Christ living in me: "It is no longer I who live, but Christ who lives in me." I take this to mean that the new self is defined by Christ's presence and help at all times. He is always imparting life to me. He is always strengthening me for what he calls me to do. That's why the Bible says, "I can do all things through him who strengthens me" (Philippians 4:13). "I toil . . . with all his energy that he powerfully works within me" (Colossians 1:29). So when all is said and done the new self says, "I will not venture to speak of anything except what Christ has accomplished through me" (Romans 15:18).

That's the first way Galatians 2:20 speaks of the new self: a Christ-inhabited, Christ-sustained, Christ-strengthened me. That's what Christ died to bring about. That's what a Christian is. The other way it speaks of the new self is this: It lives by trusting Christ moment by moment. "The life I now live in the flesh I live by faith in the Son of God, who loved me and gave himself for me."

Without this second description of the new self, we might wonder what our part is in experiencing Christ's daily help. Now we have the answer: faith. From the divine side, Christ is living in us and enabling us to live the way he teaches us to live. It's his work. But from our side, it's experienced by trusting him moment by moment to be with us and to help us. The proof that he will be with us and will help us do this is the fact that he suffered and died to make it happen.

To Give Marriage Its Deepest Meaning

Husbands, love your wives, as Christ loved the church
and gave himself up for her.
Ephesians 5:25

God's design for marriage in the Bible pictures the husband loving his wife the way Christ loves his people, and the wife responding to her husband the way Christ's people should respond to him. This picture was in God's mind when he sent Christ into the world. Christ came for his bride and died for her to display the way marriage was meant to be.

No, the point of the analogy is not that husbands should suffer at the hands of their wives. It's true, that did happen to Jesus in a sense. He suffered in order to bring a people—a bride—into being, and these very people were among those who caused his suffering. And much of his sorrow was because his disciples abandoned him (Matthew 26:56). But the point of the analogy is how Jesus loved them to the point of death and did not cast them away.

God's idea for marriage preceded the union of Adam and Eve and the coming of Christ. We know this because when Christ's apostle explained the mystery of marriage, he reached back to the beginning of the Bible and quoted Genesis 2:24, "A man shall leave his father and mother and hold fast to his wife, and the two shall become one flesh." Then in the next sentence he interpreted what he had just quoted: "This mystery is profound, and I am saying that it refers to Christ and the church" (Ephesians 5:31-32).

That means that in God's mind marriage was designed in the beginning to display Christ's relationship to his people. The reason marriage is called a "mystery" is that this aim for marriage was not clearly revealed until the coming of Christ. Now we see that marriage is meant to make Christ's love for his people more visible in the world.

Since this was in God's mind from the beginning, it was also in Christ's mind when he faced death. He knew that among the many effects of his suffering was this: making the deepest meaning of marriage plain. All his sufferings were meant to be a message especially to husbands: This is how every husband should love his wife.

Even though God did not aim, in the beginning, for marriages to be miserable, many are. That's what sin does. It makes us treat each other badly. Christ suffered and died to change that. Wives have their responsibility in this change. But Christ gives a special responsibility to husbands. That's why the Bible says, "Husbands, love your wives, as Christ loved the church and gave himself up for her" (Ephesians 5:25).

Husbands are not Christ. But they are called to be like him. And the specific point of likeness is the husband's readiness to suffer for his wife's good without threatening or abusing her. This includes suffering to protect her from any outside forces that would harm her, as well as suffering disappointments or abuses even from her. This kind of love is possible because Christ died for both husband and wife. Their sins are forgiven. Neither needs to make the other suffer for sins. Christ has borne that suffering. Now as two sinful and forgiven people we can return good for evil.

To Create a People Passionate for Good Works

*[He] gave himself for us to redeem us from all lawlessness
and to purify for himself a people for his own possession
who are zealous for good works.*

Titus 2:14

At the heart of Christianity is the truth that we are forgiven and accepted by God, not because we have done good works, but to make us able and zealous to do them. The Bible says, "[God] saved us . . . not because of our works" (2 Timothy 1:9). Good deeds are not the *foundation* of our acceptance, but the *fruit* of it. Christ suffered and died not because we presented to him good works, but he died "to purify for himself a people . . . zealous for good works" (Titus 2:14).

This is the meaning of grace. We cannot obtain a right standing with God because of our works. It must be a free gift. We can only receive it by faith, cherishing it as our great treasure. This is why the Bible says, "By grace you have been saved through faith. And this is not your own doing; it is the gift of God, not a result of works, so that no one may boast" (Ephesians 2:8-9). Christ suffered and died so that good works would be the *effect,* not the cause, of our acceptance.

Not surprisingly, then, the next sentence says, "For we are . . . created in Christ Jesus for good works" (Ephesians 2:10). That is, we are saved *for* good works, not *by* good works. And the aim of Christ is not the mere *ability* to do them, but *passion* to do them. That's why the Bible uses the word "zealous." Christ died to make us "*zealous* for good works." Zeal means passion. Christ did not die to make good works merely possible or to produce a half-hearted pursuit. He died to produce in us a *passion* for good deeds. Christian purity is not the mere avoidance of evil, but the pursuit of good.

There are reasons why Jesus paid the infinite price to produce our passion for good deeds. He gave the main reason in these words: "Let your light shine before others, so that they may see your good works and give glory to your Father who is in heaven" (Matthew 5:16). God is shown to be glorious by the good deeds of Christians. For that glory Christ suffered and died.

When God's forgiveness and acceptance have freed us from fear and pride and greed, we are filled with a zeal to love others the way we have been loved. We risk our possessions and our lives since we are secure in Christ. When we love others like this, our behavior is contrary to human self-enhancement and self-preservation. Attention is thus drawn to our life-transforming Treasure and Security, namely, God.

And what are these "good works"? Without limiting their scope, the Bible means mainly helping people in urgent need, especially those who possess least and suffer most. For example, the Bible says, "Let our people learn to devote themselves to good works, so as to help cases of urgent need" (Titus 3:14). Christ died to make us this kind of people—passionate to help the poor and the perishing. It is the best life, no matter what it costs us in this world: They get help, we get joy, God gets glory.

To Call Us to Follow His Example of Lowliness and Costly Love

*This is a gracious thing, when, mindful of God, one endures sorrows
while suffering unjustly. . . . For to this you have been called,
because Christ also suffered for you, leaving you an example,
so that you might follow in his steps.*

1 Peter 2:19-21

*Consider him who endured from sinners such hostility
against himself, so that you may not grow weary or fainthearted.
In your struggle against sin you have not yet resisted
to the point of shedding your blood.*

Hebrews 12:3-4

*Have this mind among yourselves, which is yours in Christ Jesus,
who, though he was in the form of God,
did not count equality with God a thing to be grasped,
but made himself nothing, taking the form of a servant,
being born in the likeness of men.
And being found in human form,
he humbled himself by becoming obedient
to the point of death, even death on a cross.*

Philippians 2:5-8

Imitation is not salvation. But salvation brings imitation. Christ
is not given to us first as model, but as Savior. In the experience
of the believer, first comes the pardon of Christ, then the pattern

of Christ. In the experience of Christ himself, they happen together: The same suffering that pardons our sins provides our pattern of love.

In fact, only when we experience the pardon of Christ can he become a pattern for us. This sounds wrong because his sufferings are unique. They cannot be imitated. No one but the Son of God can suffer "for us" the way Christ did. He bore our sins in a way that no one else could. He was a substitute sufferer. We can never duplicate this. It was once for all, the righteous for the unrighteous. Divine, vicarious suffering for sinners is inimitable.

However, this unique suffering, after pardoning and justifying sinners, transforms them into people who act like Jesus—not like him in pardoning, but like him in loving. Like him in suffering to do good to others. Like him in not returning evil for evil. Like him in lowliness and meekness. Like him in patient endurance. Like him in servanthood. Jesus suffered for us uniquely, that we might suffer with him in the cause of love.

Christ's apostle, Paul, said that his ambition was first to share in Christ's righteousness by faith, and then to share in his sufferings in ministry. "[May I] be found in [Christ], not having a righteousness of my own that comes from the law, but that which comes through faith in Christ . . . that I may . . . share his sufferings, becoming like him in his death" (Philippians 3:9-10). Justification precedes and makes possible imitation. Christ's suffering for justification makes possible our suffering for proclamation. Our suffering for others does not remove the wrath of God. It shows the value of having the wrath of God removed by the suffering of Christ. It points people to him.

When the Bible calls us to "endure everything for the sake of the elect, that they also may obtain the salvation that is in Christ Jesus" (2 Timothy 2:10), it means that our imitation of Christ points people to him who alone can save. Our suffering is crucial, but Christ's alone saves. Therefore, let us imitate his love, but not take his place.

TO CREATE A BAND OF CRUCIFIED FOLLOWERS

*If anyone would come after me,
let him deny himself and take up his cross daily
and follow me.*

Luke 9:23

*Whoever does not take his cross and follow me
is not worthy of me.*

Matthew 10:38

Christ died to create comrades on the Calvary road. Calvary is the name of the hill where he was crucified. He knew that the path of his life would take him there eventually. In fact, "he set his face" to go there (Luke 9:51). Nothing would hinder his mission to die. He knew where and when it had to happen. When someone warned him, on the way to Jerusalem, that he was in danger from King Herod, he scorned the idea that Herod could short-circuit God's plan. "Go and tell that fox, 'Behold, I cast out demons and perform cures today and tomorrow, and the third day I finish my course'" (Luke 13:32). All was proceeding according to plan. And when the end finally came and the mob arrested him the night before he died, he said to them, "All this has taken place that the Scriptures of the prophets might be fulfilled" (Matthew 26:56).

In a sense, the Calvary road is where everyone meets Jesus. It's true that he has already walked the road, and died, and risen, and now reigns in heaven until he comes again. But when Christ meets a person today, it is always on the Calvary road—on the way to the cross. Every time he meets someone on the Calvary road he says, "If anyone would come after me, let him deny himself and take up his cross daily and follow me" (Luke 9:23). When Christ went to the cross, his aim was to call a great band of believers after him.

The reason for this is not that Jesus must die again today, but that *we* must. When he bids us take up our cross, he means come and die. The cross was a place of horrible execution. It would have been unthinkable in Jesus' day to wear a cross as a piece of jewelry. It would have been like wearing a miniature electric chair or lynching rope. His words must have had a terrifying effect: "Whoever does not take his cross and follow me is not worthy of me" (Matthew 10:38).

So today the words are sobering. They mean at least that when I follow Jesus as my Savior and Lord, the old self-determining, self-absorbed me must be crucified. I must every day reckon myself dead to sin and alive to God. This is the path of life: "Consider yourselves dead to sin and alive to God in Christ Jesus" (Romans 6:11).

But camaraderie on the Calvary road means more. It means that Jesus died so that we would be willing to bear his reproach. "Jesus . . . suffered outside the gate. . . . Therefore let us go to him outside the camp and bear the reproach he endured" (Hebrews 13:12-13). But not just reproach. If necessary, martyrdom. The Bible pictures some of Christ's followers this way: "They have conquered [Satan] by the blood of the Lamb and by the word of their testimony, for they loved not their lives even unto death" (Revelation 12:11). So the Lamb of God shed his blood that we might defeat the devil by trusting his blood and shedding ours. Jesus calls us onto the Calvary road. It is a hard and good life. Come.

To Free Us from Bondage to the Fear of Death

Since therefore the children share in flesh and blood,
he himself likewise partook of the same things,
that through death he might destroy the one who has the
power of death, that is, the devil, and deliver all those who
through fear of death were subject to lifelong slavery.

Hebrews 2:14-15

Jesus called Satan a murderer. "He was a murderer from the beginning, and has nothing to do with the truth . . . he is a liar and the father of lies" (John 8:44). But his main interest is not killing. It is damning. In fact, he much prefers that his followers have long and happy lives—to mock suffering saints and hide the horrors of hell.

His power to damn human beings lies not in himself, but in the sins that he inspires and the lies that he tells. The only thing that damns anybody is unforgiven sin. Hexes, enchantments, voodoo, séances, curses, black magic, apparitions, voices—none of these casts a person into hell. They are the bells and whistles of the devil. The one lethal weapon he has is the power to deceive us. His chief lie is that self-exaltation is more to be desired than Christ-exaltation, and sin preferable to righteousness. If that weapon could be taken out of his hand, he would no longer have the power of eternal death.

That is what Christ came to do—take that weapon out of Satan's hand. To do this, Christ took our sins on himself and suffered for them. When that happened, they could be used no more by the devil to destroy us. Taunt us? Yes. Mock us? Yes. But damn us? No. Christ bore the curse in our place. Try as he will, Satan cannot destroy us. The wrath of God is removed. His mercy is our shield. And Satan cannot succeed against us.

To accomplish this deliverance, Christ had to take on a human nature, because without it, he could not experience death. Only the death of the Son of God could destroy the one who had the power of death. Hence the Bible says, "Since . . . the children share in flesh and blood [=had a human nature], he himself likewise partook of the same things [=took on a human nature], that through death he might destroy the one who has the power of death, that is, the devil" (Hebrews 2:14). When Christ died for sins, he took from the devil his one lethal weapon: unforgiven sin.

Freedom from fear was the aim of Christ in doing this. By dying he delivered "all those who through fear of death were subject to lifelong slavery" (Hebrews 2:15). The fear of death enslaves. It makes us timid and dull. Jesus died to set us free. When the fear of death is destroyed by an act of self-sacrificing love, the bondage to boring, bigheaded self-preservation is broken. We are freed to love like Christ, even at the cost of our lives.

The devil may kill our body, but he can no longer kill our soul. It is safe in Christ. And even our mortal body will be raised someday: "He who raised Christ Jesus from the dead will also give life to your mortal bodies through his Spirit who dwells in you" (Romans 8:11). We are the freest of all people. And the Bible is unmistakable in what this freedom is for: "You were called to freedom, brothers. Only do not use your freedom as an opportunity for the flesh, but through love serve one another" (Galatians 5:13).

So That We Would Be with Him Immediately After Death

*[He] died for us so that whether we are awake or asleep
we might live with him.*

1 Thessalonians 5:10

*To live is Christ, and to die is gain. . . .
I am hard pressed between the two. My desire is to depart
and be with Christ, for that is far better.*

Philippians 1:21, 23

*We would rather be away from the body
and at home with the Lord.*

2 Corinthians 5:8

The Bible does not view our bodies as bad. Christianity is not like some ancient Greek religions that treated the body as a burden to be gladly shed. No, death is an enemy. When our bodies die, we lose something precious. Christ is not against the body, but for the body. The Bible is clear on this: "The body is not meant for sexual immorality, but for the Lord, and the Lord for the body" (1 Corinthians 6:13). This is a wonderful statement: The Lord is for the body!

But we must not go so far as to say that without the body we can have no life and consciousness. The Bible does not teach this.

Christ died not only to redeem the body, but also to bind the soul so closely to himself that, even without the body, we are with him. This is a huge comfort in life and death, and Christ died so that we would enjoy this hope.

On the one hand the Bible talks about losing the body in death as a kind of nakedness for the soul: "While we are still in this tent [=the body], we groan . . . not that we would be unclothed, but that we would be further clothed" (2 Corinthians 5:4). In other words, we would rather move straight from here to the resurrection body with no in-between time when our bodies are in the grave. That's what those will experience who are alive when Christ returns from heaven.

But on the other hand, the Bible celebrates the in-between time, when our souls are in heaven and our bodies are in the grave. This is not the final glory, but it is glorious. We read, "To live is Christ, and to die is gain" (Philippians 1:21). "Gain"! Yes, loss of the body for a season. In a sense, "unclothed." But more than anything else, "gain"! Why? Because death for the Christian will mean coming home to Christ. As the apostle Paul says: "My desire is to depart and be with Christ, for that is far better" (Philippians 1:23).

"Far better"! Not yet in every way the best. That will come when the body is raised in health and glory. But still "far better." We will be with Christ in a way that is more intimate, more "at home." So the early Christians said, "We would rather be away from the body and at home with the Lord" (2 Corinthians 5:8). Those of us who believe in Christ do not go out of existence when we die. We do not go into a kind of "soul sleep." We go to be with Christ. We are "at home." It is "far better." It is "gain."

This is one of the great reasons Christ suffered. "[He] died for us so that whether we are awake or asleep we might live with him" (1 Thessalonians 5:10). Sleep-like, the body lies there in the grave. But we live with Christ in heaven. This is not our final hope. Someday the body will be raised. But short of that, to be with Christ is precious beyond words.

TO SECURE OUR RESURRECTION FROM THE DEAD

For if we have been united with him in a death like his,
we shall certainly be united with him in a resurrection like his.

Romans 6:5

If the Spirit of him who raised Jesus from the dead dwells in you,
he who raised Christ Jesus from the dead will also give life to
your mortal bodies through his Spirit who dwells in you.

Romans 8:11

If we have died with him,
we will also live with him.

2 Timothy 2:11

The keys of death were hung on the inside of Christ's tomb. From the outside, Christ could do many wonderful works, including raising a twelve-year-old girl and two men from the dead—only to die again (Mark 5:41-42; Luke 7:14-15; John 11:43-44). If any were to be raised from the dead, never to die again, Christ would have to die for them, enter the tomb, take the keys, and unlock the door of death from the inside.

The resurrection of Jesus is God's gift and proof that his death was completely successful in blotting out the sins of his people and removing the wrath of God. You can see this in the word "therefore." Christ was "obedient to the point of death, even death on a cross. *Therefore* God has highly exalted him"

(Philippians 2:8-9). From the cross the Son of God cried, "It is finished" (John 19:30). And by means of the resurrection, God the Father cries, "It was finished indeed!" The great work of paying for our sin and providing our righteousness and satisfying God's justice was finished in the death of Jesus.

Then, in the grave, he had the right and the power to take the keys of death and open the door for all who come to him by faith. If sin is paid for, and righteousness is provided, and justice is satisfied, nothing can keep Christ or his people in the grave. That's why Jesus shouts, "I died, and behold I am alive forevermore, and I have the keys of Death and Hades" (Revelation 1:18).

The Bible rings with the truth that belonging to Jesus means we will be raised from the dead with him. "If we have been united with him in a death like his, we shall certainly be united with him in a resurrection like his" (Romans 6:5). "Since we believe that Jesus died and rose again, even so, through Jesus, God will bring with him those who have fallen asleep" (1 Thessalonians 4:14). "God raised the Lord and will also raise us up by his power" (1 Corinthians 6:14).

Here's the connection between Christ's death and our resurrection: "The sting of death is sin, and the power of sin is the law" (1 Corinthians 15:56). Which means, we have all sinned, and the law sentences sinners to everlasting death. But the text continues, "Thanks be to God, who gives us the victory through our Lord Jesus Christ" (verse 57). In other words, the demand of the law is met by Jesus' life and death. Therefore, sins are forgiven. Therefore, the sting of sin is removed. Therefore, those who believe in Christ will *not* be sentenced to everlasting death, but will "be raised imperishable . . . then shall come to pass the saying that is written: 'Death is swallowed up in victory'" (1 Corinthians 15:52, 54). Be astonished, and come to Christ. He invites you: "I am the resurrection and the life. Whoever believes in me, though he die, yet shall he live" (John 11:25).

42

To Disarm the Rulers and Authorities

*He set aside [the legal brief against us], nailing it to the cross.
He disarmed the rulers and authorities and put them
to open shame, by triumphing over them in him.*

Colossians 2:14-15

*The reason the Son of God appeared
was to destroy the works of the devil.*

1 John 3:8

In the Bible, "rulers and authorities" can refer to human governments. But when we read that on the cross Christ "disarmed the rulers and authorities" and "put them to open shame" and "triumphed over them," we should think of the demonic powers that afflict the world. One of the clearest statements about these evil powers is Ephesians 6:12. It says that Christians "do not wrestle against flesh and blood, but against the *rulers*, against the *authorities*, against the cosmic powers over this present darkness, against the spiritual forces of evil in the heavenly places."

Three times Satan is called "the ruler of this world." Just as Jesus was coming to the last hour of his life he said, "Now is the judgment of this world; now will the ruler of this world be cast out" (John 12:31). The death of Jesus was the decisive defeat of "the ruler of this world"—the devil. And as Satan goes, so go all his fallen angels. All of them were dealt a decisive blow of defeat when Christ died.

Not that they were put out of existence. We wrestle with them even now. But they are a defeated foe. We know we have the final victory. It is as though a great dragon has had his head cut off and is thrashing about until he bleeds to death. The battle is won. But we must still be careful of the damage he can do.

In the death of Jesus, God was "canceling the record of debt that stood against us with its legal demands. This he set aside, nailing it to the cross" (Colossians 2:14; see chapter 7). This is how he "disarmed the rulers and authorities and put them to open shame." In other words, if God's law no longer condemns us, because Christ canceled our debt, then Satan has no grounds to accuse us.

Accusation of God's people was the devil's great work before Christ. The very word *Satan* means "adversary or accuser." But listen to what happened when Christ died. These are the words of John the apostle: "I heard a loud voice in heaven, saying, 'Now the salvation and the power and the kingdom of our God and the authority of his Christ have come, for *the accuser of our brothers* has been thrown down'" (Revelation 12:10). This is the defeat and the disarming of the rulers and authorities.

Now in Christ no accusations can stand against God's people. "Who shall bring any charge against God's elect? It is God who justifies" (Romans 8:33). Neither man nor Satan can make a charge stick. The legal case is closed. Christ is our righteousness. Our accuser is disarmed. If he tries to speak in the court of heaven, shame will cover his face. Oh, how bold and free we should be in this world as we seek to serve Christ and love people! There is no condemnation for those who are in Christ. Let us then turn away from the temptations of the devil. His promises are lies, and his power is stripped.

To Unleash the Power of God in the Gospel

The word of the cross is folly to those who are perishing,
but to us who are being saved it is the power of God.

1 Corinthians 1:18

I am not ashamed of the gospel, for it is
the power of God for salvation to everyone
who believes, to the Jew first and also to the Greek.

Romans 1:16

*G*ospel means good news. It's news before it's theology. News is the reporting that something significant has happened. *Good* news is the announcement that something has happened that will make people happy. The gospel is the best news, because what it reports can make people happy forever.

What the gospel reports is the death and resurrection of Christ. The apostle Paul makes the news quality of the gospel plain:

I would remind you . . . of the gospel . . . that Christ died for
our sins in accordance with the Scriptures, that he was buried,
that he was raised on the third day . . . and that he . . . appeared
to more than five hundred brothers at one time, most of whom
are still alive. (1 Corinthians 15:1-7)

The heart of the gospel is that "Christ died for our sins . . . was buried . . . was raised . . . and appeared to more than five hundred people." The fact that he says many of these witnesses are still alive shows how factual the gospel is. He meant that his readers could find some witnesses and query them. The gospel is news about facts. And the facts were testable. There were witnesses of Jesus' death, burial, and resurrection life.

The tragic thing is that, for many, this good news seems foolish. Paul said, "The word of the cross is folly to those who are perishing, but to us who are being saved it is the power of God" (1 Corinthians 1:18). This is the power that Christ died to unleash. "The gospel . . . is the power of God for salvation to everyone who believes" (Romans 1:16).

Why is the death of Christ not seen as good news by all? We must see it as true and good before we can believe it. So the question is: Why do some see it as true and good and others don't? One answer is given in 2 Corinthians 4:4, "The god of this world [Satan] has blinded the minds of the unbelievers, to keep them from seeing the light of the gospel of the glory of Christ." Besides that, sinful human nature itself is dead to true spiritual reality. "The natural person does not accept the things of the Spirit of God, for they are folly to him" (1 Corinthians 2:14).

If anyone is going to see the gospel as true and good, satanic blindness and natural deadness must be overcome by the power of God. This is why the Bible says that even though the gospel is foolishness to many, yet "to those who are called . . . Christ [is] the power of God and the wisdom of God" (1 Corinthians 1:24). This "calling" is the merciful act of God to remove natural deadness and satanic blindness, so that we see Christ as true and good. This merciful act is itself a blood-bought gift of Christ. Look to him, and pray that God would enable you to see and embrace the gospel of Christ.

To Destroy the Hostility
Between Races

He ... has broken down in his flesh the dividing wall of hostility
by abolishing the law of commandments and ordinances,
that he might create in himself one new man in place of the two,
so making peace, and might reconcile us both to God in one body
through the cross, thereby killing the hostility.

Ephesians 2:14-16

The suspicion, prejudice, and demeaning attitudes between Jews and Gentiles (non-Jews) in New Testament times was as serious as the racial, ethnic, and national hostilities in our day. One example of the antagonism is what happened in Antioch between Cephas (sometimes called Peter) and Paul. Paul recounts the story: "When Cephas came to Antioch, I opposed him to his face, because he stood condemned. For before certain men came from James, he was eating with the Gentiles; but when they came he drew back and separated himself, fearing the circumcision party" (Galatians 2:11-12).

Peter had been living in the freedom of Jesus Christ. In spite of the fact that he was a Jewish Christian, he was eating with non-Jewish Christians. The dividing wall had come down. The hostility had been overcome. This is what Christ died to achieve. But then some very conservative Jews came to Antioch. Cephas panicked. He feared their criticism. So he pulled back from his fellowship with Gentiles.

The apostle Paul saw this happening. What would he do? Serve the status quo? Keep peace between the visiting conservatives and the more free Christian Jews in Antioch? The key to Paul's behavior is found in these words: "I saw that their conduct was not in step with the truth of the gospel" (Galatians 2:14). This is a crucial statement. Racial and ethnic segregation is a gospel issue! Cephas' fear and withdrawal from fellowship across ethnic lines was "not in step with the truth of the gospel." Christ had died to tear down this wall. And Cephas was building it up again.

So Paul did not serve the status quo, and he did not maintain a gospel-denying peace. He confronted Cephas publicly. "I said to Cephas before them all, 'If you, though a Jew, live like a Gentile [non-Jew] and not like a Jew, how can you force the Gentiles to live like Jews?'" (Galatians 2:14). In other words, Cephas' withdrawal from fellowship with non-Jewish Christians communicated a deadly message: You must become like Jews to be fully acceptable. This was the very thing that Christ died to abolish.

Jesus died to create a whole new way for races to be reconciled. Ritual and race are not the ground of joyful togetherness. Christ is. He fulfilled the law perfectly. All the aspects of it that separated people ended in him—except one: the gospel of Jesus Christ. It is impossible to build a lasting unity among races by saying that all religions can come together as equally valid. Jesus Christ is the Son of God. God sent him into the world as the one and only means of saving sinners and reconciling races forever. If we deny this, we undermine the very foundation of eternal hope and everlasting unity among peoples. By his death on the cross, something cosmic, not parochial, was accomplished. God and man were reconciled. Only as the races find and enjoy this will they love and enjoy each other forever. In overcoming our alienation from God, Christ overcomes it between races.

To Ransom People from Every Tribe and Language and People and Nation

Worthy are you to take the scroll and to open its seals,
for you were slain, and by your blood you ransomed people for God
from every tribe and language and people and nation.

Revelation 5:9

The scene is heaven. The apostle John has been given a glimpse of the future in the hand of God. "I saw in the right hand of him who was seated on the throne a scroll . . . sealed with seven seals" (Revelation 5:1). Opening the scroll signifies the unfolding of world history in the future. John weeps that there seems to be no one to open the scroll. Then one of the heavenly beings says, "Weep no more; behold, the Lion of the tribe of Judah, the Root of David, has conquered, so that he can open the scroll" (5:5). This is a reference to Jesus Christ, the Messiah. He had conquered by his death and resurrection. Then John sees him: "I saw a Lamb standing, as though it had been slain" (5:6).

Then the heavenly beings around the throne fall down and worship Christ. They sing a new song. Amazingly, the song announces that it is the death of Christ that makes him worthy to open the scroll of history. The implication is that Christ's death was necessary to accomplish God's global purposes in history. "They sang a new song, saying, 'Worthy are you to take the scroll and to open its seals, for you were slain, and by your blood you ransomed people for God from every tribe and language and people and nation'" (5:9).

Christ died to save a great diversity of peoples. Sin is no respecter of cultures. All peoples have sinned. Every race and culture needs to be reconciled to God. As the disease of sin is global, so the remedy is global. Jesus saw the agony of the cross coming and spoke boldly about the scope of his purpose: "I, when I am lifted up from the earth, will draw all people to myself" (John 12:32). As he planned his death, he embraced the world.

Christianity began in the East. Over the centuries there was a major shift to the West. But increasingly now, Christianity is not a Western religion. This is no surprise to Christ. Already in the Old Testament his global impact was foretold: "All the ends of the earth shall remember and turn to the LORD, and all the families of the nations shall worship before you" (Psalm 22:27). "Let the nations be glad and sing for joy" (Psalm 67:4). So when Jesus came to the end of his ministry on earth, he made his mission clear: "that the Christ should suffer and on the third day rise from the dead, and that repentance and forgiveness of sins should be proclaimed in his name *to all nations*" (Luke 24:46-47). The command to his disciples was unmistakable: "Go therefore and make disciples of *all nations*" (Matthew 28:19).

Jesus Christ is not a tribal deity. He does not belong to one culture or one ethnic group. He is "the Lamb of God, who takes away the sin of the world" (John 1:29). "There is no distinction between Jew and Greek [or any other group]; the same Lord is Lord of all, bestowing his riches on all who call on him. For 'everyone who calls on the name of the Lord will be saved'" (Romans 10:12-13). Call on him now, and join the great global band of the redeemed.

TO GATHER ALL HIS SHEEP FROM AROUND THE WORLD

[Caiaphas] did not say this of his own accord,
but being high priest that year he prophesied
that Jesus would die for the nation, and not for the nation only,
but also to gather into one the children of God
who are scattered abroad.

John 11:51-52

And I have other sheep that are not of this fold.
I must bring them also, and they will listen to my voice.
So there will be one flock, one shepherd.

John 10:16

Without knowing it, a donkey may speak for God (Numbers 22:28). So may a preacher or a priest. It happened to Caiaphas, who was the high priest in Israel when Jesus was being tried for his life. Unwittingly he said to the leaders of Israel, "It is better for you that one man should die for the people, not that the whole nation should perish" (John 11:50). This had a double meaning. Caiaphas meant: Better that Jesus die than that the Romans accuse the nation of treason and destroy the people. But God had another meaning. So the Bible says, "[Caiaphas] did not say this of his own accord, but being high priest that year he prophesied that Jesus would die for the nation, and not for the nation only, but also to gather into one the children of God who are scattered abroad" (John 11:51-52).

Jesus himself said the same thing with a different metaphor. Instead of "children . . . scattered abroad," Jesus spoke of "sheep" outside the fold of Israel: "I have other sheep that are not of this fold. I must bring them also, and they will listen to my voice. So there will be one flock, one shepherd" (John 10:16).

Both of these ways of saying it are astonishing. They teach that all over the world there are people whom God has chosen to be reached and saved by Jesus Christ. There are "children of God . . . scattered abroad." There are "sheep not of this [Jewish] fold." This means that God is very aggressive in gathering a people for his Son. He calls his people to go make disciples, but he also goes before them. He has a people chosen before his messengers get there. So Jesus speaks of converts whom God had made his own and then brought to Christ. "All that the Father gives me will come to me, and whoever comes to me I will never cast out. . . . Yours they were, and you gave them to me" (John 6:37; 17:6).

It is an awesome thing that God looks down on all the peoples of the world and names a flock for himself, and then sends missionaries in the name of Christ, and then leads his chosen ones to the sound of the gospel, and then saves them. They could be saved no other way. Missions is essential. "The sheep hear his voice, and he calls his own sheep by name and leads them out . . . the sheep follow him, for they know his voice" (John 10:3-4).

Jesus suffered and died so that the sheep could hear his voice and live. That's what Caiaphas said without knowing it: "Jesus would die . . . not for the nation only, but also to gather into one the children of God who are scattered abroad." He gave up his life to gather the sheep. By his blood he bought the mercy that makes his voice unmistakable to his own. Pray that God would apply that mercy to you, and that you would hear and live.

To Rescue Us from Final Judgment

*Christ, having been offered once to bear the sins of many,
will appear a second time, not to deal with sin
but to save those who are eagerly waiting for him.*

Hebrews 9:28

The Christian idea of salvation relates to past, present, and future. The Bible says, "By grace you *have been saved* through faith" (Ephesians 2:8). It says that the gospel is the power of God "to us who are *being saved*" (1 Corinthians 1:18). And it says, "*Salvation is nearer to us now* than when we first believed" (Romans 13:11). We have been saved. We are being saved. We will be saved.

At every stage we are saved by the death of Christ. In the past, once for all, our sins were paid for by Christ himself. We were justified by faith alone. In the present, the death of Christ secures the power of God's Spirit to save us progressively from the domination and contamination of sin. And in the future, it will be the blood of Christ, poured out on the cross, that protects us from the wrath of God and brings us to perfection and joy.

There is a real judgment coming. The Bible describes "a fearful expectation of judgment, and a fury of fire that will consume the adversaries" (Hebrews 10:27). It calls us to live "with reverence and awe, for our God is a consuming fire" (Hebrews 12:28-29).

John the Baptist warned the people of his day to "flee from the wrath to come" (Matthew 3:7). For Jesus himself will be "revealed from heaven with his mighty angels in flaming fire, inflicting vengeance on those who do not know God and on those who do not obey the gospel of our Lord Jesus. They will suffer the punishment of eternal destruction, away from the presence of the Lord and from the glory of his might" (2 Thessalonians 1:7-9).

Some pictures of this final wrath of God are almost too terrible to ponder. Ironically, it is John, the "apostle of love," who gives us the most graphic glimpses of hell. Those who reject Christ and give their allegiance to another "will drink the wine of God's wrath, poured full strength into the cup of his anger, and . . . will be tormented with fire and sulfur in the presence of the holy angels and in the presence of the Lamb. And the smoke of their torment goes up forever and ever, and they have no rest, day or night" (Revelation 14:10-11).

Until we feel some measure of dread about God's future wrath, we will probably not grasp the sweetness with which the early church savored the saving work of Christ in the future: "[We] wait for his Son from heaven, whom he raised from the dead, Jesus who delivers us from the wrath to come" (1 Thessalonians 1:10). Jesus Christ, and he alone, can save us from the wrath to come. Without him, we will be swept away forever.

But when he saves us in the end, it will be on the basis of his blood. "Christ, having been offered once to bear the sins of many, will appear a second time, not to deal with sin but to save those who are eagerly waiting for him" (Hebrews 9:28). Sin was dealt with once for all. No new sacrifice is needed. Our shield from future wrath is as sure as the sufferings of Christ in our place. For the sake of the cross, then, exult in future grace.

To Gain His Joy and Ours

For the joy that was set before him,
[he] endured the cross, despising the shame,
and is seated at the right hand of the throne of God.

Hebrews 12:2

The path that leads to joy is a hard road. It's hard for us, and it was hard for Jesus. It cost him his life. It may cost us ours. "For the joy that was set before him [he] endured the cross." First the agony of the cross, then the ecstasy of heaven. There was no other way.

The joy set before him had many levels. It was the joy of reunion with his Father: "In your presence there is fullness of joy; at your right hand are pleasures forevermore" (Psalm 16:11). It was the joy of triumph over sin: "After making purification for sins, he sat down at the right hand of the Majesty on high" (Hebrews 1:3). It was the joy of divine rights restored: "[He] is seated at the right hand of the throne of God" (Hebrews 12:2). It was the joy of being surrounded with praise by all the people for whom he died: "There will be . . . joy in heaven over one sinner who repents"—not to mention millions (Luke 15:7).

Now what about us? Has he entered into joy and left us for misery? No. Before he died, he made the connection between his joy and ours. He said, "These things I have spoken to you, that my joy may be in you, and that your joy may be full" (John 15:11). He knew what his joy would be, and he said, "My joy will be in you." We who have trusted in him will rejoice with as much of the joy of Jesus as finite creatures can experience.

But the road will be hard. Jesus warned us, "In the world you will have tribulation" (John 16:33). "A disciple is not above his teacher. . . . If they have called the master of the house Beelzebul, how much more will they malign those of his household" (Matthew 10:24-25). "Some of you they will put to death. You will be hated by all for my name's sake" (Luke 21:16-17). That's the path Jesus walked, and that's the road to joy—his joy triumphant in us, and our joy full.

In the same way that the hope of joy enabled Christ to endure the cross, our hope of joy empowers us to suffer with him. Jesus prepared us for this very thing when he said, "Blessed are you when others revile you and persecute you and utter all kinds of evil against you falsely on my account. Rejoice and be glad, for your reward is great in heaven" (Matthew 5:11-12). Our reward will be to enjoy God with the very joy that the Son of God has in his Father.

If Jesus had not willingly died, neither he nor we could be forever glad. He would have been disobedient. We would have perished in our sins. His joy and ours were acquired at the cross. Now we follow him in the path of love. We reckon "that the sufferings of this present time are not worth comparing with the glory that is to be revealed to us" (Romans 8:18). Now we bear reproach with him. But then there will be undiminished joy. Any risk required by love we will endure. Not with heroic might, but in the strength of hope that "Weeping may tarry for the night, but joy comes with the morning" (Psalm 30:5).

49

So That He Would Be Crowned with Glory and Honor

But we see . . . Jesus, crowned with glory and honor
because of the suffering of death.

Hebrews 2:9

And being found in human form, he humbled himself
by becoming obedient to the point of death, even death on a cross.
Therefore God has highly exalted him and bestowed on him
the name that is above every name.

Philippians 2:7-9

Worthy is the Lamb who was slain,
to receive power and wealth and wisdom
and might and honor and glory and blessing!

Revelation 5:12

The night before he died, knowing what was coming, Jesus prayed, "Father, glorify me in your own presence with the glory that I had with you before the world existed" (John 17:5). And so it came to pass: He was "crowned with glory and honor *because of* the suffering of death" (Hebrews 2:9). His glory was the reward of his suffering. He was "obedient to the point of death. . . . *Therefore* God has highly exalted him" (Philippians 2:8-9). Precisely *because* he was slain, the Lamb is "worthy . . . to receive . . . honor and glory" (Revelation 5:12). The passion of

Jesus Christ did not merely precede the crown; it was the price, and the crown was the prize. He died to have it.

Many people stumble at this point. They say, "How can this be loving? How can Jesus be motivated to give us joy if he is motivated to get his glory? Since when is vanity a virtue?" That is a good question, and it has a wonderful biblical answer.

The answer lies in learning what great love really is. Most of us have grown up thinking that being loved means being made much of. Our whole world seems to be built on this assumption. If I love you, I make much of you. I help you feel good about yourself. It is as though a sight of the self is the secret of joy.

But we know better. Even before we come to the Bible, we know this is not so. Our happiest moments have not been self-saturated moments, but self-forgetful moments. There have been times when we stood beside the Grand Canyon, or at the foot of Mount Kilimanjaro, or viewed a stunning sunset over the Sahara, and for a fleeting moment felt the joy of sheer wonder. This is what we were made for. Paradise will not be a hall of mirrors. It will be a display of majesty. And it won't be ours.

If this is true, and if Christ is the most majestic reality in the universe, then what must his love to us be? Surely not making much of us. That would not satisfy our souls. We were made for something much greater. If we are to be as happy as we can be, we must see and savor the most glorious person of all, Jesus Christ himself. This means that to love us, Jesus must seek the fullness of his glory and offer it to us for our enjoyment. That is why he prayed, the night before he died, "Father, I desire that they also, whom you have given me, may be with me where I am, to see my glory" (John 17:24). That was love. "I will show them my glory." When Jesus died to regain the fullness of his glory, he died for our joy. Love is the labor—whatever the cost—of helping people be enthralled with what will satisfy them most, namely, Jesus Christ. That is how Jesus loves.

To Show That the Worst Evil Is Meant by God for Good

*In this city there were gathered together
against your holy servant Jesus . . . both Herod and Pontius Pilate,
along with the Gentiles and the peoples of Israel, to do
whatever your hand and your plan
had predestined to take place.*

Acts 4:27-28

The most profound thing we can say about suffering and evil is that, in Jesus Christ, God entered into it and turned it for good. The origin of evil is shrouded in mystery. The Bible does not take us as far as we might like to go. Rather it says, "The secret things belong to . . . God" (Deuteronomy 29:29).

The heart of the Bible is not an explanation of where evil came from, but a demonstration of how God enters into it and turns it for the very opposite—everlasting righteousness and joy. There were pointers in the Scriptures all along the way that it would be like this for the Messiah. Joseph, the son of Jacob, was sold into slavery in Egypt. He seemed abandoned for seventeen years. But God was in it and made him ruler in Egypt, so that in a great famine he could save the very ones who sold him. The story is summed up in a word from Joseph to his brothers: "As for you,

you meant evil against me, but God meant it for good" (Genesis 50:20). A foreshadowing of Jesus Christ, forsaken in order to save.

Or consider Christ's ancestry. Once God was the only king in Israel. But the people rebelled and asked for a human king: "No! But there shall be a king over us" (1 Samuel 8:19). Later they confessed, "We have added to all our sins this evil, to ask for ourselves a king" (1 Samuel 12:19). But God was in it. From the line of these kings he brought Christ into the world. The sinless Savior had his earthly origin in sin as he came to save sinners.

But the most astonishing thing is that evil and suffering were Christ's appointed way of victory over evil and suffering. Every act of treachery and brutality against Jesus was sinful and evil. But God was in it. The Bible says, "Jesus [was] delivered up [to death] according to the definite plan and foreknowledge of God" (Acts 2:23). The lash on his back, the thorns on his head, the spit on his cheek, the bruises on his face, the nails in his hands, the spear in his side, the scorn of rulers, the betrayal of his friend, the desertion by his disciples—these were all the result of sin, and all designed by God to destroy the power of sin. "Herod and Pontius Pilate, along with the Gentiles and the peoples of Israel, [did] whatever your hand and your plan had predestined to take place" (Acts 4:27-28).

There is no greater sin than to hate and kill the Son of God. There was no greater suffering nor any greater innocence than the suffering and innocence of Christ. Yet God was in it all. "It was the will of the LORD to crush him" (Isaiah 53:10). His aim, through evil and suffering, was to destroy evil and suffering. "With his stripes we are healed" (Isaiah 53:5). This is why Jesus came to die. God meant to show the world that there is no sin and no evil too great that God cannot bring from it everlasting righteousness and joy. The very suffering that we caused became the hope of our salvation. "Father, forgive them, for they know not what they do" (Luke 23:34).

A Prayer

Father in heaven, in the name of Jesus, I ask for every reader that you would confirm what is true in this book, and cancel out what may be false. I pray that no one would stumble over Christ. May no one take offense at his deity, or at his unparalleled suffering. May none reject the reasons Jesus came to die. For many, these things are new. May they be patient to consider them carefully. And would you grant understanding and insight.

I pray that the fog of indifference to eternal things would be lifted, and that the reality of heaven and hell would become clear. I pray that the centrality of Jesus in history would become plain, and that his death would be seen as the most important event that ever happened. Grant that we will be able to walk along the cliff of eternity, where the wind blows crystal-clear with truth.

And I pray that our attention would not be deflected from the supremacy of your own divine purposes in Jesus' death. Forbid that we would be consumed by the lesser question that asks which people killed your Son. All of us were involved. But that is not the main issue. Your design and your act are the main issues. O Lord, open our eyes to see that you yourself, and no man, planned the death of Jesus. And from this awesome position, let us look out over the endless panorama of your merciful, hope-filled purposes.

What an amazing truth you have revealed: "Christ Jesus came into the world to save sinners" (1 Timothy 1:15). He did it not mainly by his teaching, but by his dying. "Christ died for our sins in accordance with the Scriptures" (1 Corinthians 15:3). Is there any more wonderful message for people like us, who know we cannot measure up to the demands of our own conscience, let alone the demands of your own holiness?

Would you, then, merciful Father, grant that all who read this book see their need, and see your perfect provision in the death of Jesus, and believe? I pray this because of the promise of your Son: "For God so loved the world, that he gave his only Son, that whoever believes in him should not perish but have eternal life" (John 3:16). In Jesus' merciful name, I pray, amen.

BOOKS ON THE HISTORICAL RELIABILITY OF THE BIBLE'S RECORD

*I*f you want to read some of the best scholarship on the life, death, and resurrection of Jesus, I would recommend the following books.

Blomberg, Craig L. *The Historical Reliability of the Gospels.* Downers Grove, Ill.: InterVarsity Press, 1987.

Copan, Paul, ed. *Will the Real Jesus Please Stand Up? A Debate Between William Lane Craig and John Dominic Crossan.* Grand Rapids, Mich.: Baker, 1999.

Craig, William Lane, ed. *Jesus' Resurrection: Fact or Figment? A Debate Between William Lane Craig and Gerd Ludemann.* Downers Grove, Ill.: InterVarsity Press, 2000.

Craig, William Lane. *The Son Rises: The Historical Evidence for the Resurrection of Jesus.* Eugene, Ore.: Wipf & Stock, 2001.

Habermas, Gary R. *The Historical Jesus: Ancient Evidence for the Life of Christ.* Joplin, Mo.: College Press, 1996.

Wilkins, Michael J. and J. P. Moreland, eds. *Jesus Under Fire: Modern Scholarship Reinvents the Historical Jesus.* Grand Rapids, Mich.: Zondervan, 1996.

NOTES

1. Elie Wiesel, *Night* (New York: Bantam Books, 1982, originally 1960), p. 72.
2. Ibid., p. 73.
3. Ibid., p. 32.
4. John Newton, "Come, My Soul, Thy Suit Prepare," (1779).

desiringGod

If you would like to further explore the vision of God and life presented in this book, we at Desiring God would love to serve you. We have hundreds of resources to help you grow in your passion for Jesus Christ and help you spread that passion to others. At our website, desiringGod.org, you'll find almost everything John Piper has written and preached, including more than thirty books. We've made over twenty-five years of his sermons available free online for you to read, listen to, download, and in some cases watch.

In addition, you can access hundreds of articles, find out where John Piper is speaking, learn about our conferences, discover our God-centered children's curricula, and browse our online store. John Piper receives no royalties from the books he writes and no compensation from Desiring God. The funds are all reinvested into our gospel-spreading efforts. Desiring God also has a whatever-you-can-afford policy, designed for individuals with limited discretionary funds. If you'd like more information about this policy, please contact us at the address or phone number below. We exist to help you treasure Jesus Christ and his gospel above all things because he is most glorified in you when you are most satisfied in him. Let us know how we can serve you!

Desiring God
Post Office Box 2901 Minneapolis, Minnesota 55402
888.346.4700 mail@desiringGod.org

⊦RΘICΘL

WITH DAVID PLATT

Radical with David Platt, a half-hour national teaching program, airs daily on Moody Radio. Bestselling author, sought-after conference speaker, and pastor, David Platt brings to each program solid, passionate Bible teaching aimed at equipping and mobilizing Christians to make disciples among the nations so that the Lord receives the glory due His name.

www.radicalwithdavidplatt.org

MOODYRADIO
Where you turn. For life.

rightnow MEDIA

FREE ONLINE STREAMING OF THE
LIFE ON MISSION
YOUTH VIDEO BIBLE STUDY

FOR PURCHASING THE *LIFE ON MISSION*
BOOK, YOU GET FREE ACCESS TO THESE
BIBLE STUDY VIDEOS – PERFECT FOR
YOUTH MINISTRY OR PERSONAL DEVOTION.

TO ACCESS THESE VIDEOS FOR 90 DAYS,
VISIT RightNowMedia.org/LifeOnMission
AND USE PROMO CODE: **VFN8C3QN**

LIFE ON MISSION:
5-Session Bible Study

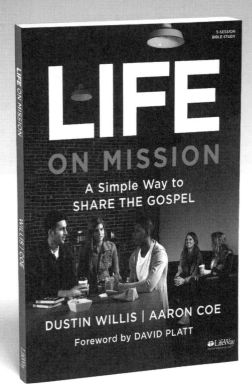

The good news of God's grace must be spoken. Other than one's own salvation, there may not be a greater joy than explaining the gospel and watching God do what only He can do: save people. We have developed a 5-week video-driven Bible study for groups. This study walks through God's heart for His mission and what it practically looks like to intentionally share the gospel.

LifeOnMissionbook.com
Releases November 1, 2014

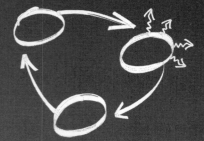

3 CIRCLES:
LIFE CONVERSATION GUIDE

Life change. It all begins with a conversation.

The gospel of Jesus Christ is the most profound reality of life. But sharing it with someone can be as simple as three circles. Discover how you can share the gospel with anyone using the Life Conversation Guide, a companion resource to the *Life On Mission* book.

sendnetwork.com/3Circles

Download the App

INTERESTED IN PARTNERING WITH SEND NORTH AMERICA?
MOBILIZE ME
namb.net/mobilizeme
NORTH AMERICAN MISSION BOARD
SEND NORTH AMERICA
namb.net

Praise for L

Willis and Coe give an inspiring and b........to the world of everyday mission. They clearly lay out before us the challenge to reach North America and offer the gospel-centered, biblical approach to how God is going to build His church through the efforts of ordinary people.

MATT CARTER, pastor of preaching, Austin Stone Community Church and coauthor of *The Real Win*

Being on mission needs to be rerouted. It has been focused on methods and models more than shaped by the gospel, God's mission, and the person of Jesus. Read *Life on Mission* and find yourself being more driven to focus your life and mission on these.

ERIC M. MASON, pastor of Epiphany Fellowship and author of *Manhood Restored* and *Beat God to the Punch*

God calls and equips His people to serve in very specific contexts related to how He uniquely gifts them. Work is worship, and I realized that early in my NFL kicking career. Done in a God-honoring fashion, work screams to a dark, hurting world there is a Creator God who intends for His children to live a full, abundant life. This book challenges me to stay living "on mission" and to know that I am His handiwork created in Christ Jesus to do very specific great works He has prepared in advance for me to do. We are all "missionaries" and Aaron helps me remember God will accomplish immeasurably more in and through me than I could ever ask or imagine when I live "life on mission."

TODD PETERSON, NFL placekicker 1993–2006
Chairman, Pro Athletes Outreach

We must be intentional, passionate, and strategic in mobilizing the church on mission. I am convinced that *Life on Mission* can help us accomplish this, resulting in accelerating our commitment to reaching our region, North America, and the world.

RONNIE FLOYD, president of the Southern Baptist Convention and pastor of Cross Church, Northwest Arkansas

A compelling book that connects mission to worship and shows how one cannot really believe the gospel and not be moved into mission. This book does more than describe mission; it compels action.

J. D. GREEAR, pastor of The Summit Church and author of *Gospel: Recovering the Power That Made Christianity Revolutionary*

The Great Commission is not for a select, elite few. It is for the whole body of Christ. *Life on Mission* makes that argument and then shows us in practical, concrete ways how to join God in His mission to make His Name famous among all peoples near and far. We all have a choice, an opportunity, to be on mission no matter who we are, where we live, or what we do. So read this book with much profit. Read it and then get to work as God's missionary in the mission field He has placed you.

DANIEL L. AKIN, president, Southeastern Baptist Theological Seminary

We are all called as leaders to be on mission as agents of the gospel, not just those in full-time ministry. *Life on Mission* defines what this looks like, how you can get there, and the good news that we all need—our lives are meant to be on mission for God! Take your next step to being on mission wherever God has placed you. Read this book!

BRAD LOMENICK, author, *The Catalyst Leader* and former president and key visionary, Catalyst

Aaron Coe is one of the most dynamic leaders in contemporary evangelicalism. This book is a theologically rooted and practically applied primer on how to join Jesus in his mission. I can think of no one with more personal credibility to challenge us in this way. This book can change your perspective, and maybe even your life.

RUSSELL D. MOORE, president, Southern Baptist Ethics & Religious Liberty Commission

Dustin Willis hits a simple message that profoundly changed my life. Focus on God's agenda while you live life and you will begin to see that people all around you are lost and in need of a Savior. This book shows us the need to pray for people in our workplace, the grocery line, soccer fields, and even in our own family. Willis and Coe provide a simple framework to love these people in a natural and friendly way that brings glory to God. This book is must-read for those that want to have purpose in their work and play.

STEVE VON FANGE, vice president information systems, Blue Cross & Blue Shield of SC

The evangelical church in North America was not built on professional mission workers and physical church buildings. It was the Holy Spirit's use of everyday Christians living on mission, knowing their context, and seeing opportunities to start ministries and churches that fueled the spread of the gospel. This book goes a long way in helping equip God's people for the work of everyday mission and ministry.

TREVIN WAX, managing editor of The Gospel Project, author of *Gospel-Centered Teaching, Counterfeit Gospels,* and *Holy Subversion.*

LIFE
ON MISSION
Joining the Everyday Mission of God

DUSTIN WILLIS | AARON COE

WITH THE SEND NETWORK TEAM

Moody Publishers

CHICAGO

© 2014 by
THE NORTH AMERICAN MISSION BOARD

All rights reserved. No part of this book may be reproduced in any form without permission in writing from the publisher, except in the case of brief quotations embodied in critical articles or reviews.

All Scripture quotations, unless otherwise indicated, are taken from the *Holman Christian Standard Bible*®, Copyright © 1999, 2000, 2002, 2003, 2009 by Holman Bible Publishers. Used by permission. Holman Christian Standard Bible®, Holman CSB®, and HCSB® are federally registered trademarks of Holman Bible Publishers.

Scripture quotations marked ESV are taken from *The Holy Bible, English Standard Version*. Copyright © 2000, 2001 by Crossway Bibles, a division of Good News Publishers. Used by permission. All rights reserved.

Scripture quotations marked NIV are taken from the Holy Bible, New International Version®, NIV®. Copyright © 1973, 1978, 1984, 2011 by Biblica, Inc.™ Used by permission of Zondervan. All rights reserved worldwide. www.zondervan.com. The "NIV" and "New International Version" are trademarks registered in the United States Patent and Trademark Office by Biblica, Inc.™

Scripture quotations marked NASB are taken from the *New American Standard Bible*®, Copyright © 1960, 1962, 1963, 1968, 1971, 1972, 1973, 1975, 1977, 1995 by The Lockman Foundation. Used by permission. (www.Lockman.org)

Edited by Ginger Kolbaba
Interior design: Erik M. Peterson
Cover design: Faceout Studio and Marcus Williamson
Cover images: Shutterstock #94785715 / #160438778 / #150875567 / #39895024

All websites and phone numbers listed herein are accurate at the time of publication but may change in the future or cease to exist. The listing of website references and resources does not imply publisher endorsement of the site's entire contents. Groups and organizations are listed for informational purposes, and listing does not imply publisher endorsement of their activities.

Some names within the text have been changed to protect the individuals' privacy.

Library of Congress Cataloging-in-Publication Data

Willis, Dustin.
  Life on mission : gospel, mission, ministry / Dustin Willis, Aaron Coe, with the Send Network Team.
     pages cm
  Includes bibliographical references.
  ISBN 978-0-8024-1221-8
  1. Missions—Textbooks. 2. Witness bearing (Christianity)—Textbooks.
3. Evangelistic work—Textbooks. I. Title.
  BV2090.W54 2014
  266--dc23
                          2014008812

We hope you enjoy this book from Moody Publishers. Our goal is to provide high-quality, thought-provoking books and products that connect truth to your real needs and challenges. For more information on other books and products written and produced from a biblical perspective, go to www.moodypublishers.com or write to:

Moody Publishers
820 N. LaSalle Boulevard
Chicago, IL 60610

3 5 7 9 10 8 6 4 2

Printed in the United States of America

DEDICATION

To the thousands of missionaries who are working hard every day to make Jesus known in North America, many of whom are doing so without great fanfare and much financial reward.

One hundred percent of the royalties from this book will go directly toward supporting missionaries in North America through Send North America.

CONTENTS

"As the Father has sent Me, I also send you."
—Jesus (John 20:21)

FOREWORD

Ordinary people with extraordinary power preaching, praying, giving, and suffering for the spread of the gospel.

This is the picture of the early church that we see on the pages of the New Testament. A small band of twelve men responded to a life-changing invitation: "Follow me, and I will make you fishers of men" (Matthew 4:19). In the days to come, they watched Jesus, listened to Him, and learned from Him how to love, teach, and serve others the same way that He did. Then came the moment when they saw Him die on a cross for their sins, only to rise from the dead three days later. Soon thereafter, He gathered them on a mountainside and said to them, "All authority in heaven and on earth has been given to me. Therefore go and make disciples of all nations, baptizing them in the name of the Father and of the Son and of the Holy Spirit, and teaching them to obey everything I have commanded you. And surely I am with you always, to the very end of the age" (Matthew 28:18–20). Just like Jesus had said from the beginning, these followers would now become fishers of men. His authoritative commission would become their consuming ambition.

Not long thereafter, they gathered together with a small group of others, about 120 in all, and they waited. True to His promise, Jesus sent His Spirit to every one of them, and immediately they began proclaiming the gospel. In the days to come, they scattered from Jerusalem to Judea to Samaria to the ends of the earth, and within one generation, they grew to over four hundred times the size they were when they started.

How did this happen?

The spread of the gospel in the book of Acts took place primarily

because ordinary people empowered by an extraordinary presence were proclaiming the gospel everywhere they went. To be sure, God did appoint well-known apostles like Peter, John, and Paul for certain positions of leadership in the church. Yet it was anonymous Christians (i.e., not the apostles) who first took the gospel to Judea and Samaria, and it was unnamed believers who founded the church at Antioch, which became a base for mission to the Gentile world. It was un-identified followers of Jesus who spread the gospel throughout all of Asia. Disciples were made and churches were multiplied in places the apostles never went. The good news of Jesus spread not just through gifted preachers, but through everyday people whose lives had been transformed by the power of Christ. They were going from house to house and in marketplaces and shops along streets and travel routes, leading people to faith in Jesus on a daily basis.

This is how the gospel penetrated the world during the first century: through self-denying, Spirit-empowered disciples of Jesus who were making disciples of Jesus. Followers of Jesus were fishing for men. Disciples were making disciples. Christians were not known for casual association with Christ and His church; instead, they were known for complete abandonment to Christ and His cause. The great commission was not a choice for them to consider but a command for them to obey. And though they faced untold trials and unthinkable persecution, they experienced unimaginable joy as they joined with Jesus in the advancement of His kingdom.

I want to be part of a movement like that. I want to be part of a people who really believe that we have the Spirit of God in each of us for the spread of the gospel through all of us. I want to be a part of a people who are gladly sacrificing the pleasures, pursuits, and possessions of this world because we are living for treasure in the world to come. I want to be part of a people who are forsaking every earthly ambition in favor of one eternal aspiration: to see disciples made and churches multiplied from our houses to our communities to our cities to the nations.

This kind of movement involves all of us. Every single follower of Christ fishing for men. Every single disciple making disciples. Ordinary people spreading the gospel in extraordinary ways all over the world. Men and women from diverse backgrounds with different gifts and distinct platforms making disciples and multiplying churches through every domain of society in every place on the planet. This is God's design for His church, and disciples of Jesus must not settle for anything less.

This kind of movement is what this book is all about. In the pages that lie ahead, Dustin Willis and Aaron Coe explain biblical foundations and explore practical implications for how God has designed your life to be a part of His purpose in the world. I encourage you not only to read this book but to apply it. And as you do, to join in what God is doing in your neighborhood, in North America and among the nations for the sake of His great name.

—David Platt

LIFE
ON MISSION

A weak gospel foundation leads to fragile mission practices.

INTRODUCTION

For almost nine years my wife and I (Aaron) served in New York City as church planters. I grew up in Kentucky in a little community outside of Louisville called Highview, which, at the time, was a three-stoplight town. Not an urban juggernaut by any stretch. My wife grew up in Oakway, South Carolina, which is home, even to this day, to one flashing stoplight. I was "uptown" and "citified" compared to her.

The New York metro area has about 22 million residents. This means approximately 27,000 people inhabit each square mile.¹ (For the sake of perspective, the state of Mississippi has about 63 people per square mile.)² So there were days when our "new" home city felt overwhelming. But we knew God had called us there for a purpose. A lot of New Yorkers don't know Jesus or attend church, and we were trying to start a church in a city that needed thousands more.

One day while walking through Manhattan, I prayed: "Lord, how are we going to reach all these people?" I felt so insignificant. I'll never forget God's answer: *Aaron, you are not going to reach New York City by yourself.* Then I felt God reveal that *He* would reach the city—by raising up hundreds of committed believers.

While lostness continues to pervade New York City and other global cities, God has chosen not to leave our communities in spiritual disrepair. He has made plans for ordinary men and women to make disciples and start churches in the unlikeliest and most unreached of places.

Maybe these churches won't be big by numerical standards or led by fully funded pastors with a paid church staff. But what I realized then and continue to see is the gospel moves forward on the shoulders of men and women willing to do the difficult work of making disciples.

By no means does Columbia, South Carolina, compare to the density and diversity of New York City, but seeing everyday, ordinary people live out God's mission is just as vital to that community. I (Dustin) will never forget examining a Columbia demographic study with the other pastors at my church. We could not shake the fact that 100,000 people within our city did not know Jesus. How could we display the gospel to every man, woman, and child? What event(s) would bring about transformation? What could we do?

Then one of the pastors laid out a map of Columbia and said, "Mark where you live." After seeing our names scattered across the map, we took this simple idea and produced an oversized map that displayed where every church member lived. We drew circles around sectors of the city where high concentrations of our members lived. We then marked dots for specific homes that could carry great influence within those neighborhoods, and then highlighted specific city blocks where we wanted to concentrate the most effort and support. While we knew that the idea of 100,000 people was not intimidating to God, seeing on a map where our members lived began to help us understand that exposing our city to the gospel was possible.

Strategically informing our people about those far from God who lived on their street or in their neighborhood and then empowering them to work together to live out the gospel with their neighbors moved us from an overwhelmed and paralyzed state to an encouraged place of movement. We realized that within our community a large event or new program wouldn't bring consistent transformation, but believers banding together to take responsibility for their dot on the map *would*.

YOUR LIFE MATTERS TO GOD'S MISSION

In the late 1930s my (Aaron) great-great-grandparents Lucinda and Samuel Clements moved from their home in Louisville, Kentucky, to an emerging suburban part of town. Upon their arrival, Grandma Lucy noticed that none of her new neighbors attended church.

Burdened by this reality she invited her neighbors to go to church with her. But when each Sunday rolled around, no one showed up. Being a feisty and persistent woman, she asked why they refused to go to church. She discovered that most of them didn't have a car or other means to travel to her church several miles away.

So Grandma Lucy determined that if her neighbors could not go to church, she would bring church to them. And in 1939, underneath a large tree in her front yard, Grandma Lucy started a Sunday school. At first, it was mostly made up of children, but over time adults began to attend too. After several years, enough people showed up that they turned that Sunday school into a church. Now, for almost nine decades, the ministry that Grandma Lucy started has been faithfully proclaiming the gospel.

It would have been easier for Lucinda Clements just to keep attending her home church, since she and my great-great-grandfather had a car. But she did not choose the easy path. As a result of her faithfulness and an understanding that her life on mission mattered, countless generations have been impacted for eternity.

The church in North America has been built by everyday missionaries such as Lucinda Clements. Throughout US history, as people settled new areas, they also started a church if one didn't exist. The Baptists had the "farmer/preacher" and the Methodists had the circuit riders. Believers understood that they were responsible to start a gospel work if none existed. As a result, in the early 1800s there was one Protestant church in the United States for every 875 people. By the beginning of World War I that ratio was one Christian church for every 430 people.[3] During that one-hundred-year span, church planting efforts significantly outpaced the population growth.

But after World War I something happened: church planting slowed

significantly. The population began to outpace new church planting and growth. Today, in places such as Alabama and Mississippi,
there's one evangelical church for about every 750 people.[4] In states
such as Indiana, Iowa, and Kansas, there is one evangelical church
for every 1,500–1,800 people.[5] In states such as New Jersey and New
York, there is one evangelical church for every 6,000–7,500 people.[6]
The Northeast Corridor and Utah have the same lack of evangelical engagement as unreached people groups, with less than 2 percent
claiming to be "born again" Christians.[7] In Canada the evangelical
presence is as low as 0.5 percent in cities such as Montreal, and Canada as a whole is only about 7 percent evangelical.[8]

As you can see, we have work to do. We have an opportunity to
pick up where previous generations have left off, but in order to do
that we need to adopt their mindset: that every believer is to live a life
on mission. No Christ-follower is exempt from using the gifts God has
given for building His kingdom.

A CHURCH ON EVERY CORNER (IS NOT ENOUGH)

Most experts say that in order to effectively impact an area with the
gospel you need to have one church for every 1,000 people in urban areas and one church for every 500 people in rural areas.[9] If you
choose to use those statistics as your guide, then many places in North
America are experiencing a significant deficit. On the other hand, just
because a church exists in that community doesn't mean it's alive and
vibrant. In the United States about 4,000 evangelical churches close
their doors every year. Of those that remain open, about 80 percent
identify themselves as plateaued, meaning that they have not seen
growth in many years.[10]

In his book *Good to Great*, author Jim Collins said that great com-
panies are those that "confront the brutal facts."[11] Well, the brutal
facts are that things are not as good for the North American church as
some might think. However, there is no need for despair. We have the
ability through the Holy Spirit's power to turn the tide—if everyone
does his or her part.

As I (Aaron) mentioned earlier, my years in New York City were at times overwhelming. The city seemed so big and impenetrable. But I believed that God was going to raise up an army of people to carry out His mission. In 2007 a group of Christians commissioned a study to look at the growth of Christianity in New York over a period of time.[12] The researchers went block by block in Manhattan to uncover the state of the church in that borough, believing it would indicate what was happening across the city. What they found was encouraging: Since 1990, Manhattan's evangelical population had grown from less than 1 percent in that year to almost 4 percent by 2007. Even more encouraging was that 40 percent of the evangelical churches had been planted since September 11, 2001. Incredible!

Here is the deal. The same God who promised to build His church in Matthew 16[13] and the one who is answering my prayers for NYC today is the same God who wants to see His church move forward on mission in your city. But this movement will not happen unless you do your part. You may not be a pastor or a church planter, but you *are* called to be something. God has equipped you uniquely to use your gifts for His kingdom's sake. The question is, are you willing to live out your calling?

SECTION 1

THE BIG
PICTURE

There is nothing more freeing than abandoning your own mission and joining the everyday mission of God.

EVERYDAY MISSIONARY

In the beginning God . . . The first words of Scripture supply for us the ultimate foundation for missions. The heartbeat of God is that He would be worshiped among all people. The writer of the Psalms conveys this sentiment when he said of God, "I will be exalted among the nations, I will be exalted in the earth!"[1] From the beginning of time in the garden, God's desire was to have a relationship with creation and for creation to see God for who He is: their Creator. As a result of the fall and sin's entrance into the world, however, humankind was inclined toward self-worship and not God-centered exaltation. Because humans' self-inclination does not square with God's righteous jealousy for His name, God is on a mission for God.[2] According to one popular writer, "Missions exists because worship does not."[3] God desires that all people worship Him and give Him the glory that is due His name.

Therefore, the mission of God requires that believers leverage their lives for His glory. The Great Commission is not for a select few; it is for the entirety of the church. The movement of God's mission sweeps across everyday, ordinary lives to draw in businesspeople, soccer moms, grandmothers, neighbors, students, lawyers, teachers, baristas, contractors, white collar, blue collar, or no collar

> Everyday missionaries are those who practice life on mission where God has placed them.

at all. Regular people like you and me united by the one who lifts the curse of the fall. Filled with His spirit, laying down our lives, denying

ourselves for the mission of God and the good of others. This is the invitation.

Welcome to the movement of life on mission. Through His church, this is God's plan to change the world.

Many people believe that mission and ministry are carried out by a select few professional clergy or an elite number of mission agencies and nonprofit organizations. But here's the reality: God's mission was given to every member of His church. We are called to be everyday missionaries. Everyday missionaries are those who practice life on mission where God has placed them, whether that be at an office complex, a developing country, or a college campus. It is incumbent on every believer to have an "all hands on deck" mentality in order for the mission to reach its fullest potential. Ephesians 4 tells us that God has given leaders to the church in order to build up His people until they "become mature, attaining to the whole measure of the fullness of Christ" (Eph. 4:13 NIV). Notice it does not say that our leaders were placed over us to do all the work. When we choose to join God on His mission through His church, we dare to be the everyday missionaries we are called to be.

> If you are a follower of Jesus, then He has a purpose and plan for you.

Your life has a mission. If you are a follower of Jesus, then He has a purpose and plan for you. But not only does God have a plan for you, Ephesians 3:20 tells us that God is able "to do far more abundantly beyond all that we ask or think, according to the power that works within us" (NASB). He wants to do more in and through you than you can imagine. Think about that: The God of the universe has a plan far beyond what your mind can conceive. What exactly does that look like? What does that mean? How will it all play out in the coming weeks and in the next five years?

MORE THAN "ME"

The purpose of God's mission isn't really about us. We live in a culture that is all about "me." Social media has allowed us to usher in the "selfie"

generation—a generation, if we aren't careful, that defines itself by self-promotion. As we begin to understand what our lives on mission are about, it is vital to understand our goals. The ultimate goal is not that we would do good things for others. It's not even to start churches or share our faith. Yes, those are good aspects of the mission, but they are not the ultimate aim. The ultimate aim of our lives is to bring glory to God.

> The ultimate aim of our lives is to bring glory to God.

If we look again at Ephesians 3:20, where we learn that God wants to do abundantly more through our lives than we can imagine, we must continue reading through verse 21, which explains the central purpose of any effort we give to God's mission. It says, "To him be glory in the church and in Christ Jesus throughout all generations, forever and ever" (ESV). One early church document tells us, "Man's chief and highest end is to glorify God, and fully to enjoy him forever."[4] The goal is glory!

The purpose of your parenting is to glorify God. The purpose of your job is to give God glory. And the purpose of your life's mission: you guessed it, to glorify God. In 1 Corinthians 10:31 it says, "Whether You eat or drink, or whatever you do, do everything for God's glory." You don't have to waste years wondering what your purpose is.

> Life on mission is about intersecting gospel intentionality into our everyday routines.

Maybe you think, *Okay, I get it. Living for God's glory is the aim, and joining God in His mission to reach my community and beyond is a means toward that great intention, but I have no idea how I'm going to add mission to the already-consistent chaos called my life.*

I (Dustin) recently participated in a conference in Austin, Texas, where I heard teacher after teacher expound on how we cannot just look at mission as something to add to our schedules but something to intersect with our current daily rhythms. Life on mission is about

> A weak gospel foundation leads to very fragile mission practices.

intersecting gospel intentionality into our everyday routines.

Adding something to the calendar can seem like an overwhelming task. God may call you to add elements, and if so, be obedient and add away. However, this book's objective is not to get you involved in some new mission program or create another church event, but rather to walk alongside you in creating a gospel intentionality within your already-present everyday rhythms.

WHAT DRIVES THE MISSION?

Living life on mission should be driven not out of guilty obligation, but rather out of embracing the identity and purpose given to us in Christ. Often, though, we are confused about our ministry motive, as well as about how to actually act on the knowledge we have. When it comes to understanding God's Word and living out God's mission, many of us tend to fall into one of three camps.

1. The "I'm not a professional" camp

Sarah represents many of us in that she rarely—if ever—takes action. She thinks she can't be a part of God's mission to redeem the world because she's not a professional minister. She equates ministry with paid professionals. She doesn't realize that *every* Christian is called to make disciples—that a Christian is necessarily a missionary in everyday life—and that her life on mission matters more than she could ever dream.

2. The "I'm too busy pondering" camp

Chris is passionate about learning as much about God as he can. He feels that knowledge about God will be his secret to his future ministry success. He loves going to seminars, reading books, and studying theology. He loves to talk about spiritual things with other believers,

but his involvement in actual ministry is minimal. He goes to church, of course, but to say he is on mission with God would be a lie. He has no intentional relationships and hasn't had a conversation with a nonbeliever in months. Though he goes "deep" in theology, he has forgotten to apply any of it to his life.

3. The "Why are we doing this?" camp

Stan, however, is the opposite of Chris. Stan is eager and task oriented. He has gotten the idea from his church that he is supposed to be active in ministry, and he has become the epitome of active. He helps with every ministry his church does, and he dutifully has conversations about Jesus with whoever will listen. But the conversations are often awkward and forced because, in reality, Stan doesn't really know what to say—he just knows he's supposed to talk. None of his words come from a legitimate overflow of meditating on the gospel and applying it to his life. They are parroted lines that he's memorized over years of familiarity with all things "church."

Chris understood the biblical foundations for ministry, but they didn't make it to his life. Stan understood the process of being a missionary, but without the biblical foundations. Too often we see people either digging deep into doctrine but never applying it, or we see those who eagerly engage in missionary activity while never digging deep into why mission work even matters. A weak gospel foundation leads to very fragile mission practices.

You don't have to fall into any of these camps because there is an altogether different option. Understanding that your life on mission matters, along with both the biblical foundations and the missionary process, is necessary to becoming an empowered everyday missionary—and the goal for this book is to train you in all three areas. Sarah will learn that she doesn't have to be a "professional" for her life on mission to matter; Stan will develop biblical foundations; and Chris will learn the practical missionary process that results from a solid biblical foundation.

A SIMPLE PROCESS

Though the need is great, through the power of the Holy Spirit, we can join God in His mission and see real change take place across North America. While mission can work itself out in many different ways, we want to offer a simple, clear process laid out in Scripture that effectively multiplies disciples and sends out everyday missionaries.

We recognize that mission and discipleship have been overly programmed and made excessively complicated, and we have no desire to do either of those. In the Scriptures, we do not see a syllabus for a program, but rather a gospel-rich missionary process.

We believe that this simple, reproducible approach, which is rooted in Jesus' example and the early church's ministry, will prove extremely effective as you follow Jesus in making disciples. The content is adaptable to any context and can function well as an individual study, but we strongly encourage walking through it with a small group of people. It is essential to interact with the content, which is threaded with powerful questions, to help you take your next steps.

We want to answer the *why, what, how, who,* and *what next* questions as you spend time working through *Life on Mission.*

- **WHY** does mission work even matter?
- **WHAT** is foundational to my growth and development?
- **HOW** do I apply the mission God has given me?
- To **WHOM** is God calling me?
- **WHAT** do the **NEXT** steps look like for me?

Our mission is driven by the truth of the gospel and defined by the mission of God. God's mission is to take what is broken and redeem it—not simply to make it better but to make it new. And the exciting part is that God Himself invites us to follow Him into a broken world as we live LIFE ON MISSION!

*When things seem bleak,
God shows up and shines
His light into the situation.*

THE CURRENT REALITY

I magine a movement of God across North America that changes the culture and attitudes of people. Imagine friends and family, once hopeless, understanding for the first time they have been given an eternal purpose that is bigger than them. Communities that are desperate being filled with courage that comes only by way of the gospel. Cities of great brokenness experiencing the newness that comes through Jesus alone.

Can you picture it?

Our role as everyday missionaries is to introduce people to Jesus, actively be part of their journey to become like Christ, and teach them to repeat the process with others. This is the desired reality, but before we move forward we must honestly examine the current reality of the mission field known as North America.

The gospel of Jesus has indeed taken root on this continent. We have historically been a land that sends missionaries to the nations who haven't heard the gospel. However, today the North American church is in decline. In his book *The Great Evangelical Recession*, John Dickerson shows that:

- Of America's 316 million people, evangelicals account for about 22 to 28 million, that means a staggering 93 percent or so are non-evangelicals.
- America's evangelical population loses 2.6 million people per decade.[1]

Denominations—from mainline to evangelical—are struggling. Consider these estimates:

- Southern Baptists report 16 million members, but only 6.1 million attend a worship service on any given Sunday.[2]
- The Presbyterian Church in America (PCA) averages one church for every 176,000 people.[3]
- The Evangelical Free Church has one congregation for every 209,333 people.[4]
- In Canada, there's one Christian Missionary Alliance church for every 81,206 people.[5]

And the list goes on.

While some evangelical denominations are on the rise, catching up with the population growth and cultural changes is another matter entirely. Here are some more statistics to consider.

- While some individual churches are growing, the evangelical numbers as a whole are shrinking, while the population is growing faster now than during the Baby Boom.[6]
- Researchers suggest that in thirty years, if the trends continue, the numbers of US evangelicals will have dropped to about 16 million, while the population will have jumped to more than 400 million.[7]

According to Outreach Canada and professor and researcher Reginald Bibby, the realities in Canada are not much better:

- Since 1980, almost three Canadian churches have closed their doors every week.
- While evangelicalism is rising above other denominations, only three in ten Canadians see religion as significant to their lives.
- The percentage of Canadian teens claiming no religion has climbed to more than 30 percent since 1980. But, Bibby says,

a majority are still keeping the door open toward spiritual things.[8]

In 2010, I (Dustin) joined some college students from the church I pastored in South Carolina and we spent a week in downtown Boston as a mission trip. One morning as I sat in a coffee shop in Boston's financial district, I pulled out my Bible to do some work on a research paper for a seminary class I was taking. A man at an adjacent table suddenly took an interest in what I was doing and the Bible that was sitting next to my computer.

"Is that a Bible?" the man asked.

"Yes," I answered. That seemed to open the door, and we began a bit of small talk about our backgrounds, family, sports, and jobs. That led to my explaining why I was in Boston.

"Wow," he said. "I've lived in Boston my entire life and I've never met a Christian out in public other than the eighteen people in my church. I've certainly never seen anyone reading a Bible at a coffee shop."

> Entire cities that were once vibrant, gospel-transformed places are now spiritually boarded-up wastelands that are far from Jesus.

The reality is, New England is now one of the most under-evangelized regions in the United States. In fact, less than 3.3 percent of this great city's population is involved in an evangelical church.[9] It's not just Boston. Entire cities that were once vibrant, gospel-transformed places are now spiritually boarded-up wastelands that are far from Jesus.

Travel five hours northeast up Highway 89 and you will find yourself in Montreal, a city that is only 0.7 percent evangelical.[10] In his article, "Overview of Montreal," Adam Miller, a writer for a major missions agency, describes Montreal as "a city with streets named after saints, with church buildings around almost every corner, but [where] things are not what they seem."[11] Montreal native and church planter François Verschelden says of his city, "Even if it seems like Jesus' presence is

here, it's not. There is a religious presence here. But His work is not known. His sacrifice is not known. Nobody can explain why Jesus died on the cross."[12]

Church buildings that once held thousands of worshipers every Sunday now serve as museums that people visit simply to observe great architecture and read placards that speak of church history. More and more church buildings are becoming new plots of real estate, lofts, and trendy concert venues. The brick and mortar of these buildings do not hold true gospel value, but the mission of the people who once populated the hallways and pews does.

On a positive side note, however, during a recent trip to Montreal, I (Dustin) learned that there are glimmers of hope. According to Jeff Christopherson, a native of Canada and mission strategist, for the last thirty years most Montreal church plants struggled to gather more than twenty-five people. But in 2013 more than six new churches were planted and each one had more than one hundred people. In fact, one church has grown to more than seven hundred people and baptized seventy new believers all in one year.

North America may have once been the center of evangelical Christianity, but that seems to be shifting to Asia, Africa, and Central America. In fact, many countries now send missionaries to North America. We praise God for the transformation taking place all over the planet, and we pray for more of it, but we must experience a resurgence of the Great Commission *here*. If the North American church grows in its gospel understanding and mission focus, the potential for what could take place all over the world grows only stronger and stronger as we send out gospel-centered missionaries, not only to our cities but also to the ends of the earth.

Can these depressed numerical trends be reversed? Is transformation possible? Is resurgence on the horizon?

How would you describe the church in North America?

CAN THESE BONES LIVE?

Declining numbers and evangelical regression can lead to frustration and mission paralysis for the church. We must remember that our God is still God and His desire for movement through His church can trump any current realities. Not sure that's true? Just look at the Old Testament prophet Ezekiel's story of how God brings life into a situation where death seems prominent.

> The hand of the LORD was on me, and He brought me out by His Spirit and set me down in the middle of the valley; it was full of bones. He led me all around them. There were a great many of them on the surface of the valley, and they were very dry. Then He said to me, "Son of man, can these bones live?" (Ezek. 37:1–3)

God showed Ezekiel a vision: a valley of dry bones—bones that were once full of life and vitality, but now lay dormant and dusty. In this vision, God breathed life into the bones and they stood as a living, breathing, and vast army.

When things seem bleak and hopeless, God shows up and breathes life into our situation. While this passage was not originally written about the North American church, the message certainly applies: Though we are a church in decline with some great needs, God can still breathe life into His church.

> When things seem bleak and hopeless, God shows up and breathes life into our situation.

How would you describe the church in your community/city?

How would you describe your church?

God has always been about forming a gospel people for a gospel mission.

THE MISSION OF GOD

I (Aaron) tend to be a take-action type of person. Actually, most personality profiles I take say, in effect, I would run over my own grandmother in a parking lot to reach a goal. When I was in college I was like most college students—broke. I remember one particular weekend I didn't have any money and it was going to be another week before I got paid from my job.

Desperate, I foraged through my house on a mission to find anything I could sell. Once I located the few items of any worth, I proceeded to move them onto the front lawn, along with a "yard sale" sign. Fortunately, I lived on a busy street and the people in my town liked to buy junk. After three hours, my take-action approach yielded me about forty dollars!

I'm not afraid to take action and neither is our culture as a whole. Too often we want to jump to the details answering the "what" and "how" questions: *What action steps must I take now? How do I do this?* But when it comes to the mission for which God has designed us, it can be dangerous to move to the "what" without asking the "why." As we push into the depths of what joining God in His mission looks like practically, we should take caution not to skip the "why," since answering that question is foundational both to our longevity and humility.

GOD'S MISSION

We read in the first chapter of Genesis that God created the world and called it good. He breathed life into humanity, the pinnacle of

creation—the very image-bearers of God.[1] Though designed to reflect Him, Adam and Eve chose self-interest over relationship with God. Genesis 3 tells the story of how they bit on the enemy's temptation and revolted against God, desiring to usurp His rule in an attempt to become gods themselves. They traded God's kingdom for their own kingdom, and it quickly crumbled.

The fabric of all creation was ripped as sin and self-immersion spread like poison to our souls. The next seven chapters of Genesis move from one devastation to the next, clearly displaying the effects of sin: deception, disobedience, and murder. The message is clear: Sin wreaks havoc.

Into this broken, bloody mess of a world, where people were reeling with pain they brought on themselves through sin, God stepped in. He chose Abram (Abraham) to become a part of His redeeming mission.

> The LORD said to Abram: "Go out from your land, your relatives, and your father's house to the land that I will show you. I will make you into a great nation, I will bless you, I will make your name great, and you will be a blessing. I will bless those who bless you, I will curse those who treat you with contempt, and all the peoples on earth will be blessed through you." (Gen. 12:1–3)

God chose to use an ordinary man like Abram (whom he renamed Abraham) to bring about change. And throughout the Old Testament God continued from Abraham to gather a people for Himself and His mission. In Exodus 19:5–6, God said that His people were a "treasured possession" and a "kingdom of priests" (ESV). A priest's job was to represent God to the people—thus making Israel a group of people who would put God on display to the nations around them. God would use them to reveal Himself to the world and press forward in the promise He made to Abraham to bless the world through his descendants.

Since the start, God's plan to bless the world was to use everyday,

ordinary people who had been reconciled to Him. This is a theme we observe not only with Abram, but with others throughout Scripture: God took men and women like Moses, Joshua, Rahab, Nehemiah, Ruth, Peter, John, and many others. And He continues that same process today. In short, God has always been about forming a gospel people for a gospel mission.

THE ULTIMATE FULFILLMENT

As we move into the New Testament, we see that not only did God choose to use an ordinary man like Abraham to bring about change, but also Abraham's bloodline eventually led to the ultimate change-agent: God in the flesh, Jesus. He is the one true priest, the one true king, and the one true prophet.

God's plan culminated in Jesus—God in human flesh, sent on a rescue mission to reconcile the world to God through the cross and resurrection. Jesus is the ultimate missionary, on task to make a people for Himself who will be a blessing, or good news, to those who are without Him. With Jesus comes the tantalizing hope of redemption—the shocking idea that maybe all is not lost and the destruction caused by sin will not have the final word.

> God has always been about forming a gospel people for a gospel mission.

After His ascension, God sent the Holy Spirit, and the church began to spread the good news of reconciliation with God through Jesus. Second Corinthians 5:18–20 tells us that as the church we have been given the ministry of reconciliation. Those of us who have been reconciled to God through Jesus now form the group of everyday people whom God uses to bless the world.

Our missionary God is not waiting for you or me—He is already at work. And the exciting news is that He invites us to join in His mission of reconciliation. The current reality of our world is certainly a motivation for what we do as everyday missionaries, but the ultimate motivator is God Himself. As we are changed and freed, we are compelled

to be where He is—right in the middle of the greatest rescue mission ever given.

How crazy is it that we are invited into this mission? Not only are we reconciled to God, but we are also drafted to be missionaries along-side Him, spreading the same good news that rescued us from our self-made destruction. We, who were convicted of treason against the King of the universe, are by grace not only forgiven but also invited into His family, adopted as His sons and daughters, and bid to spread the message of hope to other traitors.

> With Jesus comes the tantalizing hope of redemption—the shocking idea that maybe all is not lost and the destruction caused by sin will not have the final word.

What an awesome invitation that is. The fact that many Christians do not respond to the invitation reveals that many do not comprehend how good the good news of Jesus really is.

Do you believe God is calling **YOU** to be on mission with Him? If so, in what ways? If not, why not? What do you sense He is saying to you about your role?

The irony of God's kingdom is this: True fulfillment is found in sacrifice; true identity is found as we lose ourselves in Christ; and our deepest questions are answered outside of ourselves.

KINGDOM REALIGNMENT

So God is on a mission to redeem and reconcile people to Himself. This mission sweeps both history and the globe, and it encompasses regular, ordinary people like you and me. Not just the ones who give sermons, but the ones who listen. Not just paid professionals, but average Joes and Josephinas working a nine-to-five job. Not just pastors and mission agency leaders, but businessmen and soccer moms.

However, if you're honest, you may say that you don't feel much like you are part of God's grand mission. After all, it's Wednesday. Everyone despises Wednesdays. Not only do you have to get the kids ready for school, you just realized you forgot to make their lunches last night. Now you're going to be late to your meeting, and you have to figure out what you're going to tell your boss. After a crazy day at work you somehow have to figure out how to get the kids to practice on time, and you still don't know what you'll make for dinner. At this point you are just hoping to get the day wrapped up in time to kick back and watch a little television later tonight.

A missionary bearing the hope of the world is not exactly how you would describe yourself. Maybe in theory, but in practice on a random Wednesday? Your mind is far from it.

Why don't we embrace God's mission? Because, frankly, we have our own mission. We have our own way of calling the shots. We decide what's meaningful or worthwhile and order our lives accordingly. Some people's life mission is to pursue entertainment and comfort. For others it's security or wealth. For others it may be rising up the corporate

ladder or being the most respected mom in the neighborhood. We like to be the boss of our own lives.

This goes back to the sin of our first parents in the garden of Eden. As we mentioned earlier, Adam and Eve chose to be king and queen of their own kingdom rather than joyfully submitting to the authority of God as King. We may read their story in Genesis 3 and shake our heads, but the fact is that we have all done the exact same thing in one way or another. In light of this, it's not surprising that some of Jesus' first words in His earthly ministry were: "Repent, because the kingdom of heaven has come near!" (Matt. 4:17).

Repent. That word stings our pride, but once we get past that, we realize it oozes with grace because it invites us into something better. Repent, because the kingdom already has a King, and you and I are not it.

If we are ever going to get swept up into God's kingdom, we will have to let go of our own. Our own ways of seeing and approaching our lives will have to be radically reoriented.

THE GOOD NEWS OF THE KINGDOM

In twenty-first-century United States, we don't exactly have the perfect context for *king* and *kingdom* language. In large part we are more familiar with democracy, in which every voice counts equally. For the vast majority of people throughout history, however, the language of monarchy would ring with weight, because it's exactly what they lived in. In their world if a king decreed something, it happened. No questions asked. If the king wanted something to become a law, it became a law. There was no system of checks and balances to make sure the king didn't become a tyrant.

The idea of living under a monarchy might seem unappealing because you know plenty of stories where power and authority corrupt and cause unthinkable damage. But the hesitation that arises when thinking about living under a solitary king or queen's rule lessens when you realize that the goodness (or badness) of living under such authority depends entirely, and we mean 100 percent, on the goodness (or badness) of the said king or queen. What would you think of

living under a perfectly good, perfectly wise King whose every decision was for your benefit and eternal good? That may in fact not be so unappealing.

Throughout His ministry, Jesus' message resounded with the truth that His kingdom had come, and that it was a kingdom of good news—not a kingdom of oppression and corruption. Who wouldn't want to live in that kingdom? Matthew 4:23 states that Jesus went all over Galilee "preaching the good news of the kingdom." Truly understanding this idea of good news begs some context.

Historically, during a time of war, kings would set off to battle for their people against the given enemy. If the king was defeated, his people would either become slaves to the enemy or be killed. Messengers would run back to the city yelling, "Run for your lives!"

However, when the king and his soldiers triumphed, he would send back a messenger to let the people know that the enemy had been defeated. The messenger would yell, "Good news! Good news!" This could have literally meant freedom from impending slavery or death. This news from the messenger is the same word we now use as the word *gospel*, which in its simplest form means, "good news."

The message of King Jesus is the gospel. Our King has gone before us and defeated the enemy, therefore imparting to us victory over the slavery of sin and death. This is no everyday good news—this is life-altering good news, and we who have been reconciled to God have now been given the privilege of spreading this good news to a world that is in desperate need of it. The good news of the kingdom is that God doesn't leave us in a state of sinful devastation, but calls us to turn from our sin and to look to Him for hope and restoration.

For the remainder of this chapter, let's look at why it is good news that Jesus is the King of His kingdom.

GOOD NEWS: JESUS IS ON THE THRONE

Several years ago I (Aaron) traveled to England for a conference. While there I took a day to see London. The last stop on my tour was at Buckingham Palace, home to Queen Elizabeth. The tour guide

> The King is on His throne reigning over His kingdom.

explained the tradition behind the changing of the guard and many of the other historic symbols. One especially memorable remark was about the significance of the flag on top of the palace. The guide explained that when the queen is not in residence, the flag does not fly. Though the Queen of England does not have the official power over the people that she once held, there is still a strong sense of national pride and security in knowing that she is there. For the people of England, when the flag is flying, the people can be assured that the queen is on her throne!

When looking at the decline and challenge facing the North American church (as we discussed in chapter 2), the task of the mission can seem daunting. However, we cannot allow any amount of hopelessness or despair to gain control over us. Why? Because the King is on His throne reigning over His kingdom.

From the beginning, God has reigned over the universe. Regardless of what the world tells us, that hasn't changed. He has always been the sovereign King of the cosmos, with ultimate rule and reign, and He will continue to be nothing less. He is the King of kings on a mission. He reminds us that whenever we read Matthew 16:18: "I . . . say to you that you are Peter, and on this rock I will build My church, and the forces of Hades will not overpower it."

The fact that God is on His throne and that Jesus is building His church should bring us great relief. We can release any unnecessary pressure or worry that ministry may tempt us to carry and trust that God *will* accomplish what He has set out to do.

GOOD NEWS: JESUS IS A DIFFERENT KIND OF KING

When you think about earthly kings and queens, odds are you may think about some faraway, inaccessible royalty who is unable (or simply uninterested) to relate to his subjects. You may think of an aloof and uncaring ruler who has only his own best interests in mind.

But Jesus is an altogether different kind of king. He took on the

very plight of His subjects to provide a way out of the mess they had made for themselves. He is far from aloof, uncaring, or inaccessible, someone who does not meddle in the affairs of His people. Jesus is a King who got down into the mess of humanity, who went to ultimate lengths to seek and save the lost and restore people back into His kingdom. Jesus is the best King imaginable, because He is that perfectly wise and good King who always works everything for the best for those who love Him and are called according to his purpose.[1]

> Jesus is a King who got down into the mess of humanity, who went to ultimate lengths to seek and save the lost and restore people back into His kingdom.

Since Jesus is a different kind of king, we serve in a different kind of kingdom. The kingdom of God takes what culture tells us and turns it upside down. The more we grow in knowing this good King, the more the truths of an upside-down kingdom become real. Take a look at these cultural "norms" and how they compare to God's kingdom.

WHAT CULTURE SAYS: Be first.

WHAT GOD SAYS: The last will be first and the first will be last (see Matt. 20:16).

WHAT CULTURE SAYS: Step over others to exalt yourself.

WHAT GOD SAYS: Humble yourself to be exalted (see Matt. 23:12, James 4:10, 1 Peter 5:6).

WHAT CULTURE SAYS: Do whatever makes you look best.

WHAT GOD SAYS: Take the worst seat at the table instead of the best (see Luke 14:8–10).

WHAT CULTURE SAYS: Your life is what's most important.

WHAT GOD SAYS: Consider others better than yourself (see Phil. 2:3–4).

WHAT CULTURE SAYS: Always get/do what you want.

WHAT GOD SAYS: Die to your own desires (see Luke 9:23).

WHAT CULTURE SAYS: Take care of yourself first and foremost.

WHAT GOD SAYS: Whoever loses his life will find it (see Matt. 16:25).

WHAT CULTURE SAYS: Maybe forgive, but don't forget.

WHAT GOD SAYS: Love and pray for your enemies (see Matt. 5:44).

WHAT CULTURE SAYS: Have nothing to do with those who are against you.

WHAT GOD SAYS: Bless those who persecute you (see Rom. 12:14).

WHAT CULTURE SAYS: No one tells you what to do.

WHAT GOD SAYS: Go further than what you are asked (see Matt. 5:41).

> It is truly a good kingdom, with a good King, with good news for a hurting world.

The irony of the kingdom is that: (1) True fulfillment is found in sacrifice; (2) True identity is found as we lose ourselves in Christ; (3) Our deepest questions are answered outside of ourselves. It is truly a good kingdom, with a good King, with good news for a hurting world.

GOOD NEWS: THE KINGDOM IS ALL ABOUT JESUS

The reason our personal kingdoms feel so small is because . . . well, they are. No part of who we are is big enough to merit the weight and grandeur of a king because only one life is. The writer of Hebrews put it this way:

Long ago God spoke to the fathers by the prophets at different times and in different ways. In these last days, He has spoken to us by His Son. God has appointed Him heir of all things and made the universe through Him. The Son is the radiance of God's glory and the exact expression of His nature, sustaining all things by His powerful word. After making purification for sins, He sat down at the right hand of the Majesty on high. So

He became higher in rank than the angels, just as the name He inherited is superior to theirs. (Heb. 1:1–4)

Here's an exercise for you. Answer the following questions based on the above passage:

1. By whom has God spoken to us?
2. Who is the heir of all things?
3. Through whom did God make the universe?
4. Who is the radiance of God's glory?
5. Who is the exact expression of God's nature?
6. Who sustains all things by His powerful Word?
7. Who purifies us from all sin?
8. Who is seated at the right hand of the Majesty?
9. Who is ranked higher than the angels?

If you grew up in and around the church, you know that the answers to the above questions are all the same and typically viewed as "Sunday school answers." In other words, if you don't know the answer while sitting in a building with stained glass windows, then simply say, "Jesus," and there is a good chance you'll answer the typical "Sunday school question" correctly. The answer really is that simple, though—Jesus. The kingdom really is all about Jesus—about who He is, what He has done, and what He continues to do as King.

Jesus is the one through whom God has spoken to all of humanity. *Jesus* is the King and heir with God the Father of all things. *Jesus* is the one through whom God the Father made the universe. *Jesus* is the exact expression of God's nature. *Jesus* is the radiance of God's glory. *Jesus* sustains all things by His powerful Word. *Jesus* purifies us from all our sin. *Jesus* is seated on the throne at the right hand of the Majesty.

Jesus is not only the King, creator, sustainer, and brilliance of God's glory, but also the means by which sinful man can be made clean again. It's good news that the kingdom is all about Jesus, because

worshiping Him is what all of creation was designed for. Reflecting God's glory is the only thing that will ever truly satisfy and enliven not only us as humans, but the very grass, oceans, rocks, and trees that cover the earth.

GOOD NEWS: JESUS IS A SERVANT KING

Throughout the New Testament we see over and over how Jesus served others. One poignant scene, in particular, is when He washed His disciples' feet (see John 13:1–17). But the apostle Paul shows a more profound portrait of Jesus as a servant King:

> Christ Jesus, who, existing in the form of God, did not consider equality with God as something to be used for His own advantage. Instead He emptied Himself by assuming the form of a slave, taking on the likeness of men. And when He had come as a man in His external form, He humbled Himself by becoming obedient to the point of death—even to death on a cross. For this reason God highly exalted Him and gave Him the name that is above every name, so that at the name of Jesus every knee will bow—of those who are in heaven and on earth and under the earth—and every tongue should confess that Jesus Christ is Lord, to the glory of God the Father. (Phil. 2:5–11)

Jesus completely turns our natural ideas about power, authority, and privilege upside down. The world values ascending whatever success or popularity ladder there happens to be nearby, while Jesus values descending to serve the least of those among us. His descent from heaven to save and serve us is our great motivation and example to humble ourselves and serve those around us. In the standard economy of a kingdom,

> Jesus is not only the King, creator, sustainer, and brilliance of God's glory, but also the means by which sinful man can be made clean again.

kings are not servants and servants are not kings, yet King Jesus is both. We have an all-powerful and mighty God who purifies us from our sin not by sitting idly by, but rather by exalting Himself through becoming the Servant King.

GOOD NEWS: WE GET TO REPENT

Jesus calls us to repent of building our own kingdoms, which is good news because kingdom realignment is the best thing that could ever happen to us. Before moving to the practical nature of living on mission we must first examine our hearts. Instead of living to pursue our own pleasure and attain our own glory—which is always fleeting—we get to be swept up in the greatest story that's ever been told and glorify the true and rightful King Jesus with our lives. He gives us a new and better purpose—one that will never fade or fail us—even in eternity and even on a Wednesday. Chasing after His fame and glory instead of our own is the best trade we could ever make.

> In the standard economy of a kingdom, kings are not servants and servants are not kings, yet King Jesus is both.

The kingdom of God is a real kingdom—not a sand castle like our meager attempts. We are not only invited into God's kingdom, we are also invited to be part of spreading the good news. We get to "plead on Christ's behalf, 'Be reconciled to God' " (2 Cor. 5:20).

The wayward are not lost forever. *King Jesus seeks and finds them.*

The traitors who chose treason over relationship are not hopeless after all. *King Jesus reconciles them to the Father.*

The prisoners and mourners are not left in their despair. *King Jesus breaks the chains of sin and grants freedom while giving comfort to the hurting.*

The poor and brokenhearted are not left by the wayside. *King Jesus restores us through kindness and transforms us to be spiritually rich.*

Indeed, it is a kingdom of good news. But we only have the opportunity to spread this news and plead on His behalf when we practice

kingdom realignment—when we leave behind our own kingdoms and pursue His. And this kingdom realignment leads us to a kingdom mentality, where, as everyday missionaries, we are more concerned with the bigger picture of God's kingdom than we are with ourselves.

In times past, how have you seen your life realign with God's kingdom purposes?

In what ways do you still need to surrender your kingdoms to Him?

LIFE
ON MISSION

GOSPEL FOUNDATIONS

The gospel is not something you simply "get." It is something you grow deeper in throughout your life.

THE GOSPEL

A life on mission is a calling of abandonment. It is the confession of our willingness to set aside—to abandon—our preferences to follow God's mission. Like a bungee jumper diving off a platform, we must relinquish our selfish hopes with total abandon to spread the true hope we have found in Jesus.

And like the bungee jumper, we soon discover that what once may have seemed dangerous or unappealing becomes the thrill of a lifetime once we let go. Living out a gospel mission is not a guilt- or fear-driven task—it is the good life. Author Tim Chester says, "The secret of gospel change is being convinced that Jesus is the good life and the fountain of joy. Any alternative would be the letdown."[1] We realize the good life as we see Jesus for all He is and follow Him without hesitation.

From birth we hold firmly on to things. Once a baby learns to hold a bottle, there is no going back to Momma and Daddy holding it. This pattern continues throughout life. A number of months ago my wife and I (Dustin) taught our two-year-old daughter, Piper, to use a spoon to feed herself. Now, if I even hint like I'm going in the direction of her spoon, she acts as if I have deeply offended her and attempts to send me to "time out." I think, *You're two. You get lost in your own room. Chill out.*

A teenager begins driving and it's as if he's cursed if he has to submit to riding with his parents ever again. And as adults we hold firmly to what we achieve—great job, financial success, beautiful house—as if that's all we have. It becomes the singular banner over our lives.

However, when we take on the mind of Jesus, we hold on to our plans and ideals loosely. We become more willing to follow His plans and ideals, even if on the surface they don't make sense and may not seem successful. The point is that we become willing to hold our plans in an open hand rather than a closed fist.

Several years ago my wife, Carmen, and I (Aaron) felt God calling us to adopt a child. After several attempts and upon discovering that more than fifteen thousand NYC foster children needed homes, we enlisted a social-worker friend to help us navigate the bureaucratic system and lead us to become "foster parents with the intention to adopt." We knew that fostering to adopt domestically would be a complicated endeavor. We had heard horror stories of those who had done it only to have a child taken away abruptly.

A few weeks after completing our foster care training, Joshua came to live with us. Joshua was six weeks premature. He spent his first twenty-two days in the hospital (most of that time in the Pediatric Intensive Care Unit). On the day Joshua came into our home he weighed just a little more than four pounds. The social workers brought him in a carrier and set him on our living room floor. They took a box of diapers and formula and set them on the kitchen counter. No instruction manual. No time to warm up to him. In a period of about eight minutes we became parents of a little boy.

As the social workers were leaving, one of them stopped and said, "By the way, Joshua has a sister in foster care. She's about eighteen months old. Would you take her too?"

Our child, plus Joshua, and now a third one? All under the age of four. Were we crazy? In that moment, my wife and I should have said no. Everything within us—our own desires and realities—wanted to say, *This one is* more *than plenty*. But through the power that can come only from the Holy Spirit, we looked at each other and said yes. And a few months later, Ella joined our family.

When Carmen and I entered the adoption process, we'd visualized how it would go. We thought we would get one child through a closed, foreign adoption. Instead we've ended up with two children

through domestic foster care. And though we've had our fair share of complications (as of this writing we're still waiting on the official adoption paperwork, four years into the process), we're thankful for the process God has taken us through, as He has used it to shape our attitudes and plans to align more with Christ's. God has proved that His plans are higher and greater than anything we can conjure up on our own. We just have to trust Him.

FIRST IMPORTANCE

Our ability to trust Jesus and hold our plans loosely is not built on our own merits. Being an everyday missionary is impossible without a solid foundation. The gospel is like that bungee cord that keeps the jumper connected to life, and our missions efforts are in vain if we are without our "gospel" cord. We must not jump off the platform without being securely fastened to the gospel of Jesus, because there is no other hope for us or for our aching world. An everyday missionary who is not grounded in the gospel is no missionary at all because he or she does not have good news to proclaim. Every other religious idea in the world primarily gives advice for one's life, whereas the gospel is an announcement of good news that *transforms* a life.

> The gospel is not something you simply "get." It is something you grow deeper in throughout your life.

Over the last decade, the word *missional* has grown in popularity. For the most part, this has been a great thing for the church, but there is potential danger if we don't have a clear understanding of what should always determine and drive the mission set forth for us. If we don't grow in the gospel, we will not get the mission.

Before you think, *I get the gospel, I know the gospel, I know why I'm on mission,* remember: The gospel is not something you simply "get." It is something you grow deeper in throughout your life.

This chapter lays the groundwork for the rest of the content you will read. You should consider jumping back to this chapter from time

to time as a reminder of what our mission is built upon. Theologian Charles Hodge said, "The gospel is so simple that small children can understand it, and it is so profound that studies by the wisest theologians will never exhaust its riches."[2] The more we dig into its depths, the richer this transforming news becomes.

If the gospel is not genuinely the foundation and motivation of our mission, we will likely falter and lead others astray. The more we grasp what Jesus has done for us and in us, the more we will be compelled by grace to clearly communicate Jesus to those around us.

Aaron and I (Dustin) have served as student/college pastors during our time as ministers, and, without fail, we've noticed a perpetual cycle of students who participate in mission work because it makes them feel good about themselves. These same students then head to college or into the workforce and leave the idea of a relationship with Christ back at their summer mission trip. Unfortunately, for many the motive for missions isn't the gospel—it is a guilt- or works-based mentality, built on the idea that we can somehow erase our sin or earn favor with God by doing the "right" things. To believe that our mission efforts in some way eradicate sin isn't much different from an Eastern-based karma belief with a splash of Jesus.

This reality is true not only for students, but also for many others in our churches, whether they wear a three-piece suit or a V-neck and skinny jeans. It is often that folks in the pews or chairs will "do" the periodic mission service project but leave the "real" mission work Monday through Friday to the hired "professional." Our mission efforts are vital and must increase as we move toward a more progressively post-Christian era, in which our values and worldviews are no longer based in the Christian faith. Our motivation for mission has to be that Jesus is already our great reward. When taking the risk of living selflessly on mission, we must be grounded and affixed

> The gospel is the starting point, the sustaining point, and the finishing point of all missions—to all of life.

to that gospel understanding. So the gospel is the starting point, the sustaining point, and the finishing point of all mission—to all of life. In 1 Corinthians 15:1–4 Paul wrote:

> I want to clarify for you the gospel I proclaimed to you; you received it and have taken your stand on it. You are also saved by it, if you hold to the message I proclaimed to you—unless you believed for no purpose. For I passed on to you as most important what I also received: that Christ died for our sins according to the Scriptures, that He was buried, that He was raised on the third day according to the Scriptures.

The gospel of Jesus is of greatest importance. It applies to and affects everything (work, school, leadership, friendships, marriage, family). It is the ultimate game-changer.

Think about why you participate in mission work. What are some things that motivate you (e.g., compassion for the poor, experiencing new cultures, sharing the gospel)?

How do you consider yourself "sent" from God? Is there room for growth in your view on missions? How? Why?

How do you define the gospel?

List ways the gospel affects every area of your life (work, relationships, school, etc.) and your mission work.

Life: _____

Mission: _____

GOD'S HOLINESS AND GREATNESS

As created beings, we are measured and defined by comparison to our Creator. We cannot truly understand ourselves without first looking

at the awe-inspiring holiness and majesty of God.

In Isaiah 6, the prophet found himself standing in heaven. He saw the Lord sitting high on a throne, His robe filling the temple. Angels surrounded Him, singing, "Holy, holy, holy is the LORD of hosts; His glory fills the whole earth." While they sang, the foundations of the doorways shook and the temple filled with smoke.

This passage, among many others, describes the overwhelming "otherness" of God. He is completely holy; set apart, transcendent, all knowing, all powerful. He is the one and only true God, the creator and sustainer of all things, the one in whom all things "live and move and exist" (Acts 17:28). Being altogether righteous and holy, God cannot look upon or tolerate sin (see Hab. 1:13). It is an affront to His majesty, His character, and His design for life. Grasping and digesting the character of who God is will help us better understand the depths of the grace He has for us.

Spend a few minutes now to describe your understanding of the nature and character of God.

OUR SINFULNESS

As Isaiah saw God sitting on His throne, angels worshiping Him, while the foundations shook because of the weight of His glory, Isaiah had an immediate and gripping response: "Woe is me for I am ruined because I am a man of unclean lips and live among a people of unclean lips, and because my eyes have seen the King, the LORD of Hosts" (Isa. 6:5).

This was not a religious spectacle or some rote spiel spouted from memory. In this moment, in the presence of an all-holy God, Isaiah was overwhelmed by his own sinfulness. That reality is not the most exciting to own up to, but it's true to its core and necessary in order to grasp the full depth of the gospel. Every facet of our existence—even our so-called "good" works—is shot through with sin. Because of this, we are separated from God and rightfully under condemnation.

This is the reality of our human character:

- Even what we view as "good" works is viewed as polluted garments compared to God's goodness (see Isa. 64:6).
- We suppress the truth when we exchange the creator God for the created things of this world (see Rom. 1:18–25).
- By nature and choice, we are not good. Only God is good and we choose in and of ourselves not to fear or pursue Him (see Rom. 3:9–20).
- Our hostility leads toward evil deeds and further separation from God (see Col. 1:21).

Describe your understanding of the nature and character of humanity.

How is our nature and character different from God's?

What do you sacrifice for the most? What do you daydream about? ("If I just had more _____, I'd be happy.")

Where do you spend your time and money most frequently? In what do you tend to seek significance, worth, value, and acceptance?

The only way to truly evaluate ourselves is through an honest view of God's holiness and our own sinfulness. Like Isaiah, we have to look first at God to see ourselves clearly. How would you answer these statements?

God is holy, and I am _____.

God is forgiving, and I am _____.

God is generous, and I am _____.

God is caring, and I am _____.

God is alive, and I am _____.

If you wonder what should be written in the blanks above—the word *not* will suffice, when we are absent the grace of God. Sin is not just a setback or obstacle to overcome, it is a self-inflicted curse—a cancer we can do nothing in and of ourselves to remedy. As Louie Giglio stated, "Sin doesn't make us bad, sin makes us dead. The gospel doesn't make us better, the gospel makes us alive."[3]

As you know, our hearts are more than surface deep. Often deeper, underlying motivations are really driving our behaviors. If we are ever going to achieve true freedom from sin, we have to let God dig down to the roots of it.

For example, Gary was struggling with severe alcohol addiction and began attending a recovery ministry at my (Dustin's) church. Gary explained that he had a serious problem with alcohol for almost a decade, but he always thought he had it under control—until the previous weekend. He had taken friends to party at a strip club, only to wake up the next morning hung over and $6,000 poorer. This was a wake-up call for Gary and he finally realized he needed help. Interestingly before they even talked about idolatry in the recovery ministry, Gary explained it well: "You know, it's not even about the alcohol, or about lust. I'm a really nice drunk. People like me when I'm drunk. I'm generous. So when I go out with my friends and tell them to do whatever they want and the tab is on me, it makes me feel powerful and liked. That's the real issue. That's really why I do it."

Without realizing it, Gary had explained that his surface sin of alcohol and lust were really the deeper issues of approval and power. Isn't that fascinating? Our sin is deep and multifaceted, and it requires a deep and multifaceted cure.

Consider some of the sins you struggle with, and ask yourself why. What is the deeper reason you turn to these things? Ask the Holy Spirit to help you understand your true motivation.

But we don't stop at our sin. There is great news for those who recognize the hopelessness of their state, those who with Isaiah cry, "Woe is me!" That news is the boundless hope of grace.

"BUT GOD"

What happened to Isaiah is gratefully a foreshadowing of the gospel.

> Then one of the seraphim flew to me, and in his hand was a glowing coal that he had taken from the altar with tongs. He touched my mouth with it and said: "Now that this has touched your lips, your wickedness is removed and your sin is atoned for." Then I heard the voice of the Lord saying: "Who should I send? Who will go for Us?" I said: "Here I am. Send me." (Isa. 6:6–8)

After Isaiah was stunned by God's holiness, then overwhelmed by his own sinfulness, God stepped in to intervene in what felt like a hopeless situation. The burning coal from the altar symbolizes the cleansing, atoning work of Jesus applied to us by grace through faith.

It has been said that the two best words in the Bible are found in Ephesians 2:4: *But God*. In verses 1–3 of that chapter, we see the overwhelming weight we all feel, just as Isaiah did, when we are separated from God. These two words, *But God*, form the transition from the bad news of sin and condemnation to the unbelievable good news of forgiveness through Jesus: "*But God*, who is rich in mercy, because of His great love that He had for us, made us alive with the Messiah even though we were dead in trespasses. You are saved by grace!" (Eph. 2:4–5, emphasis added).

The reason we have hope is because God is rich in mercy. Mercy is simply God's compassion for the undeserving. The word *rich* in the above passage is the same word used to describe a wealthy king who has more money than he knows what to do with. That is how much mercy God has for us. His grace and mercy abound, proving to be more than sufficient for our many shortcomings. As Lamentations 3:22–23 says, His mercies "are new every morning." Pastor and author Tim Keller states, "The gospel is that Jesus lived the life you should have lived and died the death you should have died, in your place, so God can receive you not for your record and sake but for His record and sake."[4]

Throughout Scripture God is described as loving and compassionate, and this Ephesians passage grounds the saving work of Christ in the "great love that He had for us." Though we are more sinful than we'll ever truly know, we are *still* loved by God more than we could ever imagine.

"But God" is truly incredible news!

THE PRESSURE IS OFF

When I (Dustin) was pastoring in Columbia, South Carolina, one of our pastors, Brandon, met regularly with a young man named Jason. Jason struggled with a severe addiction to pornography that had plagued him for years. Over several months as they talked, Brandon realized there was more going on than sexual sin.

Jason kept expressing that he had a lot of anxiety over his obedience to God, or lack thereof. He said it was difficult for him even to hear grace-based sermons because he was consumed by feelings of failure.

"No matter what I do, I can't seem to be good enough," he would say. "I can't hit the proverbial ball right—even in the little things, like reading my Bible and praying. I constantly feel anxious and helpless."

Brandon noticed that Jason completely missed the gospel because he was so focused on his own performance, so he started to remind Jason of one of the gospel's basic tenets: We are affirmed and approved by God based on Jesus' performance, not our own.

"I have a new mantra for you, Jason," Brandon told him during one of their sessions. "*The pressure is off.* If Jesus is your Savior, the pressure is off. There is no need to perform. You are already forgiven, approved, and affirmed based solely on Jesus' righteousness. And there is *nothing* you can do to add or take away from Jesus' righteousness." Slowly but surely, that simple truth started to work freedom into Jason's soul.

The gospel is not based on what you do for God, but what God has done for you. It is not "you do" but "Jesus did." Sadly, this works-based righteousness is second nature to us, simply because of pride. We want to be good enough. We want to measure up on our own. Even mission and ministry can be turned into a performance for God—an act to

try to win His favor or affirmation. This is a dangerous subconscious ideology that leads to destruction, and we must be freed from it by continually going back to the gospel and reaffirming that we are already approved in Jesus, so there's no need to earn it.

How do you struggle with turning mission into a performance for God?

GROWING IN THE GOSPEL

The gospel is not only the *starting* point, it is also the point in *every* step of our journey. The gospel is how we become Christians, but it is also how we grow as believers—through meditating on it and applying it to every fabric of our lives.

When my (Dustin's) son, Jack, was three years old, he and I found ourselves making a pizza run in the ever-hospitable traffic that is Atlanta. It was around 5:30 p.m., and if I'm being completely vulnerable, I'm not sure whether Atlanta's rush-hour traffic was leading toward my sanctification or my madness. In an attempt to distract myself from the bumper-to-bumper surroundings, I asked my son a simple question.

"Jack, what is the gospel?"

From his car seat he looked directly into the mirror where he could see the reflection of my face and said, "The gospel is good news. Right, Daddy?"

"Yeah, son, that's right. But what is the good news?"

"The good news is that we get grace."

I pressed further. "Okay, but what is grace?"

He rolled his eyes as if to say, *Seriously, Dad, everybody knows that.* Then he said, "Grace is getting what we don't deserve."

As those words came out of his mouth, I thought, *I've got a little theologian on my hands. This is incredible.*

He went on to say, "You know, Daddy, when I deserve a time-out and you don't give me one? That's grace."

My son recently pushed his little sister down, quickly looked at

> The gospel is not based on what you do for God, but what God has done for you. It is not "you do" but "Jesus did."

me, and said, "Grace, Daddy, grace." To which I replied, "It's time to learn about justice. Justice, son, justice."

Nonetheless my son impressed me on this drive to grab a pizza. I wanted to dig a bit more so I asked him, "Okay, so we get what we don't deserve, but how do we get that? What had to take place?"

Quickly and emphatically he said, "Jesus died on the cross." There was an aggressive growl to his voice when he said "cross."

"That's right. But what did Jesus die for?" Finally, he seemed stumped as I continued to weave my way through the crazy traffic, all the while commenting on how people need to learn to drive: "Get out of the left lane. Move over!"

He thought long and hard, and said, "Hmmm, Daddy. Jesus died for your bad attitude."

I wish I could have taken a snapshot of the grin he wore that moment. His statement was not only hilarious, but the Holy Spirit used it to communicate and affirm in me a life-changing truth.

The gospel is not exclusively about salvation, but also about our sanctification, our becoming more and more like Jesus. The transforming nature of the gospel is that God, through the power of His grace, continually changes us to be like Jesus, even in our bad attitudes while driving to pick up a pizza.

If the gospel truly applies to every area, and our calling is to live life on mission, then we must examine, marinate, and apply the full truth of this great news.

You might think that the good news of Jesus grows less meaningful and prevalent as in time you move away from the point of your conversion, but the opposite is actually true. If you walk in honesty and confession, allowing the Holy Spirit to search your heart deeper and deeper, you realize quickly that your heart gets uglier the deeper you delve.

Not only do we struggle with wrong actions and behaviors, but with wrong thoughts, motivations, and desires. This causes us to grow more aware of our need for grace, and the work of Jesus becomes

bigger in scope and importance as we see the growing necessity for it.

EVERY FABRIC

I (Dustin) like using a red pen to go back through my journal and mark the places where I've seen circumstances change or where I have seen God move. This is a great practice, but leaving that red pen in your jeans pocket and then tossing the jeans into the washing machine is a terrible mistake—unless you hope for new red-themed attire.

I have learned firsthand, and to my wife's great disappointment, that if a person releases a single drop of potent red dye into a load of laundry, that dye will run its course until every stitch of fabric is red. Terrible news for clothes, but great illustration for how the good news of Jesus affects our lives in an all-encompassing way.

Author Dave Harvey stated, "The gospel is the heart of the Bible. Everything in Scripture is either preparation for the gospel, presentation of the gospel, or participation in the gospel."[5] The summation of the Scriptures is the message of the gospel; therefore, the gospel should transform every fabric of our lives. It reaches every facet of our being and leaves nothing untouched. Jesus doesn't make us halfway new, He makes us fully new.

Grasping the colossal contrast between God's holiness and our sinfulness leads us to a clearer view of what truly is so amazing about grace. And that will lead us down a path of reflecting His compassion to others as we mature and grow in the gospel.

So let's look back at the statements from page 65 and replace the word *not* with a new phrase.

Our reality absent of God's grace says: God is holy, and I am **NOT**. But a grace-filled reality says: God transforms me to be **HOLY** (see 1 Peter 2:9).

Our reality absent of God's grace says: God is forgiving, and I am **NOT**. But a grace-filled reality says: God transforms me to be **FORGIVING** (see Col. 3:13).

Our reality absent of God's grace says: God is generous, and I am **NOT**. But a grace-filled reality says: God transforms me to be **GENEROUS** (see 2 Cor. 8:8–15).

Our reality absent of God's grace says: God is caring, and I am **NOT**. But a grace-filled reality says: God transforms me to be **CARING** (see 1 Peter 5:1–7).

Our reality absent of God's grace says: God is alive, and I am **NOT**. But a grace-filled reality says: God transforms me to be **ALIVE** (see Col. 2:13).

HUMBLE CONFIDENCE

Understanding God's grace leads us more and more to a place of humble confidence—humbled by the weight of our sin and need for salvation, yet confident that in Jesus we have all the grace, mercy, approval, and affirmation we will ever need. His work really is sufficient. God does not love us any more or less based on our performance or lack thereof, so we can humbly bring every fabric of our lives out into the light.

Hebrews reminds us: "For we do not have a high priest who is unable to sympathize with our weaknesses, but One who has been tested in every way as we are, yet without sin. Therefore let us approach the throne of grace with boldness, so that we may receive mercy and find grace to help us at the proper time" (Heb. 4:15–16).

What implication does Hebrews 4:15–16 have for your life?

Your community and the people God puts in your path need to be exposed to people who are holy, forgiving, generous, caring, and alive. This type of person isn't self-made, but transformed. The gospel of Jesus is the only means by which this type of person is possible. It's through grace and *grace alone*.

Where does the gospel need to be applied to your life in this moment?

THE GOSPEL FUELS THE MISSION

Take a look back at Isaiah 6 from earlier in this chapter. The timeline of events is insightful. Isaiah didn't run off to the mission field after realizing his own sin, hoping that working for God would somehow make up for his wickedness, and thus earn God's approval.

However, as Isaiah encountered a powerful foreshadowing of the gospel—being cleansed and having his sin atoned for—he became a changed man. He also became a compelled man. When God called out, "Who should I send? Who will go for Us?" Isaiah, compelled by grace, quickly volunteered himself by saying, "Here I am. Send me." The grace of God had humbled him, changed him, given him hope, and moved him. It then became a compelling force, calling him outward toward God's mission. And God can do the same for you.

How does God's grace fuel your mission?

Our world does not simply need people who know more facts about God, but rather people who are falling deeper in love with who God is.

CHAPTER 6

SPIRITUAL MATURITY

There are two things they put in the hands of Kentucky boys when they are born: a bottle and a basketball. Basketball is a year-round obsession for the state. When I moved to Tennessee for college, I (Aaron) was astonished that people actually cared about football. In Kentucky we used football to get us in shape for basketball season.

From the time I was small, I played basketball. By my sophomore year of high school I was on the varsity team. Though I was becoming a good individual player, our team wasn't very good. During my sophomore and junior years we won just fourteen out of sixty games.

My senior year we got a new coach, and everything changed. This coach had been an assistant at the University of Kentucky under Rick Pitino and chose to start his coaching career at our high school (his alma mater).

I'll never forget our first practice. He told us the reason we'd been so bad was that we had a bunch of head knowledge about basketball but didn't execute on that knowledge. For the first hour or so of practice he repeated to us the fundamentals of basketball, and he told us that we would concentrate on getting those right before we moved to more complicated aspects of the game.

For the first time in a long while, our team gained both knowledge about the game and how to practically execute that knowledge. That combination led to a massive change that season. We won twenty games and made it to the district finals for the first time in our school's history.

In a similar manner, long-term success in our given life mission is dependent upon our spiritual growth and maturity. Having a knowledge of theology is great if we are taking a test, but that amounts to zero if we don't apply it. Theology applied to everyday life through the Spirit of God at work in us, however, results in spiritual maturity. This Spirit-led growth is essential in order to live a successful, enduring life on mission.

THE MATURITY GAP

In Hebrews 5:11–14, the author told the recipients that although they should be teachers by now, they still needed someone to teach them the basics about God. Instead of being able to eat solid food, the author said that the people still needed milk as would infants who cannot feed themselves. The image is an alarming one, prompting us to picture an older child or even adult who still drinks formula from a bottle.

One truth that the author related in Hebrews 5 is that although there should be a correlation between the amount of time a person has known Jesus and their spiritual maturity, it doesn't always work that way. There are many believers whose maturity falls way behind their spiritual age. At times there is a gap of jarring proportions.

So what can we do for those who fall behind in spiritual maturity? The image from Hebrews 5 again rings true—we have to start where that person is spiritually. Milk has to come before solid food, and if their lives do not show that they have grasped the basics of Christianity (the "milk"), then we go back to the basics.

BASIC #1: THE SUPREMACY OF GOD

One of the marks of a person who is spiritually maturing is that they have a big view of God. They have come to trust that He is King and able to do what He says He will do.

It is important to understand that God is at the center of His mission and that, by default, as we discussed in chapter 4, we are not. If we believe that God is supreme, then we are in a good position to

mature spiritually. Our desires and decisions will be in submission to Him, fostering a lifetime of repentance and realigning our hearts toward His heart and kingdom.

A big view of God is the starting point for mission. Paul understood this when he prayed his desire for the church at Ephesus, that they be able to understand the "breadth and length and height and depth" of the love of God.[1] He knew that a deep understanding of God would result in a deeper faith. Throughout Scripture the people who were used in the greatest capacities were the ones who had a high view of God.

Nehemiah had a big view of God. Upon hearing of Jerusalem's destruction, he appealed to his "great and awesome" God prior to approaching the Persian king to ask permission to go rebuild the city walls—knowing full well that such an approach would mean risking his life.[2]

Similarly, Queen Esther knew that her life could be ended if she approached the Persian king about aiding in the plight of the Jews, her people. However, after prayer and fasting, her view of God emboldened her toward her calling to a royal position "for such a time as this." If it cost her life, she believed, so be it.[3]

And we can't overlook the apostle Paul's view of God. In Acts 9, Paul encountered the risen Jesus, which radically altered his life's trajectory. He moved from persecuting the church to being persecuted for the church.

What would cause a person to risk his or her life for the sake of the mission? It is an unwavering belief in the God of the mission. Missional "pep talks" or guilt sessions will not ultimately make you satisfied in your life on mission; only a robust picture of God will enable this type of action. Theology professor Keith Whitfield supports this idea: "We will not be able to recover a vision and passion for missions until we recover the grandeur that God made us to know and worship Him and make Him known throughout the whole earth."[4]

As we seek to mature, we must consider the supremacy of God and be drawn to reflect upon the attributes that make Him supreme. As we

consider and personalize those attributes, a maturity of faith in who God is becomes more pronounced.

BASIC #2: THE SOVEREIGNTY OF GOD

God is sovereign. God is involved in every aspect of His creation from providing food for us (see Matt. 6:11) to knowing the number of days we will live (see Ps. 139). All of our talents are a result of God's goodness to us (see 1 Cor. 4:7). Author Wayne Grudem says that David understood that his military skill came from God when he wrote in Psalm 18 that "he trains my hands for war so that my arms can bend a bow of bronze."[5] An everyday missionary must understand that God is at work in the world and is asking His children to respond in obedience to that work. It is not up to us to determine the focus of our mission; it is up to us to follow God. This should come as a huge relief since God has not left us alone in the missionary enterprise.

The fact that God is sovereign should give us hope that as long as we follow in obedience, we are in the center of God's will. There will be many days on our journey when things will not seem to go right. Walking through personal kingdom realignment and joining the everyday mission of God is not a simple and clean process. Everyday mission is messy. It will not always go as planned. People will reject us. We will say the wrong thing at the wrong time and often conversations will become more difficult before they become easy. Walking through the messiness of mission with the right perspective can act as a breeding ground for spiritual maturity. We may be tempted to think that somehow we have missed God's plan. But it is in those moments, if we are faithful, that we can trust we are right where we are supposed to be.

James 1:2 (ESV) says that we are to "count it all joy . . . when [we] meet trials of various kinds." Experiencing joy in the midst of trials is a sign of spiritual maturity, and the only way a person can have joy in the midst of hardship is to know that the sovereign one who commands joy will be faithful to deliver on His promises.

Many of us live under the weight of failure because our success metrics are derived from the wrong source. Understanding God is in

control of all things will work as a great starting point toward freedom from those metrics and, ultimately, grow us toward maturity. And a sign of that maturity is accepting that God is sovereign over your mission. There is not one ounce of it that He has not orchestrated.

BASIC # 3: THE LOVE OF GOD

God is loving. From third-grade Sunday school onward, you probably understood that "God so loved the world."[6] Why does God love and why should that love help develop maturity and propel us toward mission?

In God's act of creation recorded in Genesis, we see that when God created people, He created them in His "image," and He referred to His creation as "very good." So from the beginning a distinctive relationship existed between the Creator and His creation. As we have already highlighted in chapter 3, by Genesis 3, people had rebelled against the Creator and ushered sin into the world.

Because of His holiness, God had every right to banish humanity from the face of the earth (as we discussed in chapter 5). But He chose not to do that. In a mysterious act of grace, He chose to have mercy on His people and pursue a relationship with them. In the Old Testament this relationship manifested itself in God's covenant with Israel. In the New Testament, God's covenantal relationship with Israel came to completion through Christ's work on the cross—and not only for Israel, but for *all* people. In that one act, Christ, who knew no sin, became sin for the people. He took upon Himself God's wrath, which was intended for the people. This was His greatest act of love toward His creation. That understanding allows us to clearly see that His mission—and ours—is not the result of duty, but the result of his great love for us (see Eph. 2).

Any time we consider God's wonders, it further deepens our faith in who He is. We increasingly recognize our need for Jesus and the cross (see John 3:30). That lends itself to more maturity, which in turn makes us more and more passionate about the things of Christ, such as consistently reading and meditating on the Scriptures (see

Rom. 10:17 and Ps. 119:11), regularly spending time with God in prayer (see Luke 11:5–9), and serving the poor, the marginalized, the despised, and the imprisoned (see Matt. 25:35–36).

As we continue to comprehend more and more who God is and who we are in Christ, and as a result we apply that understanding to every aspect of our lives, then we reach the very essence of what it means to grow in spiritual maturity. As Jesus continues to transform our hearts and as we submit our sinful nature to the Holy Spirit's work, spiritual maturity will be consistently present. While this does not mean we will be perfect or even near perfect, we will see evidence of heart change and a more Christlike attitude.

MATURITY AND CHANGE

The gospel doesn't just free you, it changes you. In Galatians 5, Paul gave us a picture of what the change in our lives will look like when we are being molded by the Holy Spirit.

> The fruit of the Spirit is love, joy, peace, patience, kindness, goodness, faith, gentleness, self-control. Against such things there is no law. Now those who belong to Christ Jesus have crucified the flesh with its passions and desires. Since we live by the Spirit, we must also follow the Spirit. (Gal. 5:22–25)

When we walk with Jesus, we consistently develop more and more of these characteristics (or fruit). As we spend time with Him, confess our sin to Him, and surrender our wills to Him, our hearts will actually change. It won't simply be white-knuckled behavior modification—no, it will be deep-down, soul-level change. When circumstances heat up and the "real" you comes out, there will be a marked difference from the way you would have reacted in the past to that situation. Fruit is what comes off of a tree and it can't be faked. The same is true with spiritual fruit—it is only the result of Holy Spirit–led maturity and heart change.

Take Jared and Tammy, for example. They are active in their church

and have been Christians for about ten years. For many years, their marriage was a wreck. They would have knock-down, drag-out fights that would often end with one of them leaving. But since becoming believers and seeing how the gospel applies to their marriage, Jared and Tammy are slowly but surely seeing their marriage transformed. They still argue, but where unbridled pride and self-interest had been present, there is now humility. Where defensiveness, anger, and harsh words were once rampant, there is a spirit of gentleness and understanding. Where the works of the flesh once took control, now the fruit of the Spirit (see Gal. 5:22–25) is growing and evident.

Both of them are fighting for the humility to see themselves as the "worst of sinners"[7] in their marriage (see 1 Tim. 1:15). They realize that through the gospel, they have been forgiven so much, and that realization fuels them to forgive each other. They look first to the log in their own eyes before pointing out the speck in the eye of the other (see Matt. 7:1–5). Their kids no longer run for cover when they hear the first hint of disagreement.

As Jared and Tammy seek Jesus through prayer and Scripture, their lives are changing. Their marriage is a testament to God's grace instead of a monument to sin's destruction. They realize that if God is supreme, His design for life and marriage is trustworthy. They understand that in God's sovereignty they were led to each other for both their sanctification (growth in the gospel) and God's glory. They are "the one" for each other not because the other is perfect, but because they are married to each other. They have also come to understand that all of this—their marriage, their faith, and their entire lives—is nothing but evidence of God's great love for them.

KNOWING VERSUS APPLYING

Who would you say is more mature: the person who knows a hundred things about God and applies one of them, or the person who knows two things about God and applies both? In reality, the person who knows only two things but applies both things would be more mature, right?

Many of us tend to define spiritual maturity by how much knowledge a person seems to have. If someone owns big books by dead guys, quotes Scripture in every conversation, and throws around Greek or Hebrew every now and then, they certainly give off an air of maturity, don't they? But unfortunately, knowledge does not equal maturity.

Humility, obedience, and mercy are far more closely tied to maturity. Holding our lives up as clay to be molded and shaped by God and His truth is the real mark of maturity. One of my (Dustin's) mentors in college, Dwight Robertson, consistently told me, "The greatest gift we can give the world around us is our closeness with God." Our world does not simply need people who know more facts about God, but rather people who are falling deeper in love with who God is and applying His truth to everyday life.

How would your life be different if you were to begin applying the basic truths about God to your life? How would the lives of those around you be different?

What does spiritual maturity look like to you?

Reread Galatians 5 (found on page 80 in this chapter). Write a short three- to four-word description of each of the fruit of the Spirit. Which ones do you see strongly in your life? Which ones do you still need work on?

Pray for growth in each of these areas as they are a picture of spiritual maturity.

We need one another to carry out the mission of God.

BIBLICAL COMMUNITY

L iving in a city (Columbia, South Carolina) that is in a humid subtropical climate does not lend itself to a plethora of winter storms, but on the rare occasion that it snows, the place shuts down. On one of those infrequent occasions the snow and ice rolled into our unprepared southern city, and the heating system failed for one of my (Dustin's) neighbors.

Addie was a college-age girl who had been attending our church gatherings and lived a couple streets over from me. When her rental house's heat broke down, she and her roommates crashed at our house. My wife is gifted in hospitality so having them stay with us was a treat: a lot of sledding, hot chocolate, soup, and conversations.

They stayed with us three days, and during that snow-venture Addie began to open up to my wife and me about her past and the deep pain and veiled scars she had carried around. Addie had been sexually abused by a family member for most of her young life. Through her tears she described how her view of what a father should be and how a family should love had been shattered. My wife and I were heartbroken for her and could see that this was one of the first times this guarded girl had told of her agonizing past. As she continued to make herself vulnerable, we experienced the beginnings of an arduous healing process.

In the months and years to come, our church family loved her and cared for her as our sister. Not only did we get to experience the different stages of healing with her, but we had the blessing of watching God

use her story and the power of biblical community to bring restoration and redemption for others.

Years after our snow-mageddon (I'm pretty sure it was little more than a dusting) had long melted away and right before God called my wife and me to move to Atlanta, we received a handwritten letter from Addie. It was meek and poetic, and even now as I reflect on it my eyes are filled with tears.

Addie explained how her fragmented portrait of family became redeemed through the simple but effective mission that comes by means of biblical community. She wrote simply how she knew now what family was and how, through the community of her new brothers and sisters, she had learned she has a heavenly Father who can be trusted and who loves her deeply.

She said that though the wounds of her past still carried a sting, God was slowly but surely making her new and that all had started through the redemption of understanding what community could and should be. She closed the letter with the simple phrase, "Thank you for being my family. We have a good Dad, don't we?"

This is a picture of biblical community: being part of the family of God and working together so that people see a clear portrait of who God can be as their Father. As believers we may not be in the same family bloodline, but Ephesians 2 explains how we all share in the uniting truth that we have been blood-bought and adopted into a family with God Himself as our Father. Biblical community is woven into the fabric of living as an everyday missionary.

At that time you were without the Messiah, excluded from the citizenship of Israel, and foreigners to the covenants of the promise, without hope and without God in the world. But now in Christ Jesus, you who were far away have been brought near by the blood of the Messiah. For He is our peace, who made both groups one and tore down the dividing wall of hostility. In His flesh, He made of no effect the law consisting of commands and expressed in regulations, so that He might create in Himself one

new man from the two, resulting in peace. He did this so that He might reconcile both to God in one body through the cross and put the hostility to death by it. When the Messiah came, He proclaimed the good news of peace to you who were far away and peace to those who were near. For through Him we both have access by one Spirit to the Father. So then you are no longer foreigners and strangers, but fellow citizens with the saints, and members of God's household, built on the foundation of the apostles and prophets, with Christ Jesus Himself as the cornerstone. The whole building, being put together by Him, grows into a holy sanctuary in the Lord. You also are being built together for God's dwelling in the Spirit. (Eph. 2:12–22)

God has reconciled believers to Himself and adopted them as sons and daughters into His family. As God's children, the church is designed to function as a family, united in heart and purpose. Biblical community is built upon committed, authentic, and caring relationships that urge one another toward Jesus and His mission. God never intended for us to live out the Christian life alone.

> God never intended for us to live out the Christian life alone.

Together as believers we make up the body of Christ and operate as a picture of gospel transformation to the world in which we exist. Foundationally, everyday missionaries understand their biblical calling to be anchored to a group of believers, to whom they confess, with whom they repent, celebrate, live in faith, and are daily sent out on mission.

Here are some characteristics of people who are connected to biblical community:

- They have people with whom they are honest and transparent about their struggles with sin (see James 5:16).
- They gracefully confront sin in other believers and humbly accept correction brought by others (see Gal. 6:1–2).

- They willingly sacrifice in order to help others carry their burdens (see Gal. 6:2).
- They celebrate and see the value of God's unique giftedness and life experiences within each individual (see Rom. 12:6–8).
- They practice hospitality that helps nurture relationships (see Heb. 13:2).

COMMUNITY: NON-NEGOTIABLE

A solitary faith is not a Christian faith.

Our North American culture places high value on independence and individualism, so it can be difficult for us to understand the necessity of community. *Why can't it just be me and Jesus?* we think, toting our Bibles off in some lone-ranger mission to save the world.

The problem is, you can't choose Jesus and not choose the church. They are a package deal. And by church we don't mean a group of people you sing songs and listen to a sermon with once a week. That is certainly one of the valid expressions of church and one we should be consistently involved in, but going to a service once a week is not walking in biblical community. Biblical community is the group of believers with whom we walk through the good, the bad, and the ugly of life while digging deeper into the gospel.

We are given many commands in the New Testament about living out our faith. Sometimes these are referred to as the "one another" commands. And they all deal with the idea of living a life on mission through community. Here are a few of them:

- Love one another (see John 13:34).
- Show family affection to one another (see Rom. 12:10).
- Outdo one another in showing honor (see Rom. 12:10).
- Accept one another (see Rom. 15:7).
- Serve one another through love (see Gal. 5:13).
- Carry one another's burdens (see Gal. 6:2).
- Be kind and compassionate to one another, forgiving one another (see Eph. 4:32).

- Encourage one another (see 1 Thess. 4:18).
- Confess your sins to one another and pray for one another (see James 5:16).
- Be hospitable to one another (see 1 Peter 4:9).
- Clothe yourselves with humility toward one another (see 1 Peter 5:5).

God is not simply putting more to-dos on our list to make the Christian life more difficult, but rather He is using these foundational tools to grow us toward our own spiritual maturity and to further His mission in the world. The beautiful thing is that as we obediently pursue these commands, Christ is put on display to those around us. We actually become the body of Christ, as we are called in the New Testament.

Recently a popular Christian writer wrote a blog post on why he rarely attends church anymore. His rationale was that he had "graduated" from church and had found other ways to connect with God. Specifically, he said that it was through his work that he found his deepest God-connection.

Though we understand the sentiment, it is not remotely close to being biblical. Throughout the New Testament, particularly in Romans 12 and 1 Corinthians 12 and 14, we see that Christ-followers are all given different gifts (serving, teaching, exhortation, etc.) to exercise *within* biblical community. Every place in Scripture where we observe a spiritual gift, we always find it in a collective list with other spiritual gifts that other individuals may possess. Spiritual gifts are not about individuals but purposed to build and edify the church and its mission. This means that the church is designed to be interdependent, working together toward one uniting mission. If one rogue member "graduates" from the body, then the body will not function with one another as it should—and the rogue member won't either.

THE MESSINESS OF "ONE ANOTHER"

So how can you practice these "one another" commands by yourself on your lone-ranger mission? You're right, you can't. And you're not

meant to. Community is your support system, your sustaining grace when you need encouragement, prayer, rebuke, or help with a struggle. To be sure, while biblical community is an essential part of Christian living, it can be extremely arduous. Real relationships are messy and you can get hurt. Listen, I (Dustin) received my undergrad degree in marketing, so I realize the above statement is not the most attractive to tell people when you want them to become an involved Christian.

The church is a bunch of sinful people getting together with a bunch of sinful people working out sinful lives and believing that God will somehow use it all to grow the group toward maturity. Sounds like a crazy idea, but that is the mystery of how the Holy Spirit works—through imperfect people. I'm sure nine out of ten people reading this book have been hurt by someone in the church, and the tenth person is simply in denial. But as we embrace the messy tension that is community, with its call for patience, grace, and perseverance, God will build His kingdom. Just because community is difficult doesn't give you an "out" option.

Just like soldiers in the army, biblical community is the people you walk into battle with—the people who will get in your face when you need it. It is the circle of brothers and sisters with whom you do life, reminding one another consistently of the grace we so desperately need.

So why are we so often resistant to walking in the light of community? Jesus answers this question in John 3:19–21.

This, then, is the judgment: The light has come into the world, and people loved darkness rather than the light because their deeds were evil. For everyone who practices wicked things hates the light and avoids it, so that his deeds may not be exposed. But anyone who lives by the truth comes to the light, so that his works may be shown to be accomplished by God. (John 3:19–21)

In short, we are prideful people. We don't like to expose our failures and weaknesses, and we like to pretend we have our acts together. But

as Hebrews 4:13 reminds us: "No creature is hidden from Him, but all things are naked and exposed to the eyes of Him to whom we must give an account.".

How have you seen the "one another" commands lived out in your community? How did they put the body of Christ on display for you and others around you?

NO MORE HIDING OR PRETENDING

Isn't trying to hide from God and others exhausting? The good news of the gospel is that God fully knows us—down to our darkest moments; yet He loves us more than we could ever imagine. So we don't have to put on a façade; we are free to walk out into the light of reality.

If we are truly accepted in Jesus, then we can be honest with others and not put on a show to try to win their approval. If we have been forgiven by Jesus, we can forgive others. If we understand that our righteousness has been accomplished by Jesus, we are free to stop trying to earn it on our own abilities.

Community is essential because it is one of the primary ways we grow in the gospel. If we don't practice the "one anothers" and live honestly and openly, we simply don't have the opportunities to apply the gospel. We fake it, and our growth is phony.

Yes, community can be tough, but what are you waiting for? Your righteousness has been accomplished in God. Step out of the obscurity of delusion and into the freedom of honesty. The more we lean into that honesty, the more we start to see how numerous our imperfections really are—which is a sign of maturity. As we observe our sin, it can lead us to confession.

When you hear the word *confession* what comes to your mind? First John 1:5–10 explains how walking in the light allows us fellowship with others and that God has forgiveness waiting on us. We simply need to confess our sin. How good is *that* good news? God has forgiveness ready for us. All we have to do is honestly say, "I'm wrong." Confession can be one of the most freeing practices. James 5:16 tells

us there is healing when we confess and allow others to pray for us. We can all think of a time where we worked hard to conceal a sin, until finally we reached the breaking point and confessed it. Remember how freeing that felt? That relief is the truth of James 5:16 directly touching us. And that's part of biblical community: applying God's love and forgiveness to our relationships.

What and how does that challenge your view of confession?

FRONT YARDS, BREAKING CARS, AND LIVING ON MISSION

When my wife and I (Dustin) moved to Atlanta, God blessed us with an incredible avenue for mission, also known as our neighborhood. We regularly invite our neighbors plus families in our church community group to cookouts in our front yard. We are intentional about inviting our community group because (1) we want to encourage other Christians to engage with their neighbors; (2) we know that some people may have greater connection with our neighbors than we do; (3) we desire to display Jesus through our group to our neighbors.

That plan has been a blessing. For instance, my neighbor Andrew is a car maniac. He's the kind of guy that if nothing is wrong with his car, he will break something simply to have something to work on.

I know nothing about cars. When I take my car to a mechanic, I'm the guy who makes sounds to describe what's wrong with it. I am every mechanic's dream client. However, Clay from my community group knows cars, and through one of the neighborhood cookouts, Clay and Andrew struck up a conversation. They now hang out on a regular basis, talking cars and on occasion talking gospel. Andrew said recently, "You and your friends really care about one another. You guys are like family. It's just different."

Andrew's not a Christian yet, but he is seeing Jesus through biblical community. Jesus said in John 13:35, "By this all people will know that you are My disciples, if you have love for one another." The way we relate to one another can put the gospel on display in much the

same way as a service project does in a city. Our intentionality in loving one another plays a foundationally vital part in living out our everyday mission.

Who are you wrestling alongside through the truths of the gospel? Who's confronting you in your sin? Who are you confronting? Who are you confessing to? Who are you walking in repentance with? Who are you learning the idea of forgiveness from? Who are you partnering with to live out mission?

Take a few minutes and list the people you are or should be living out the gospel with. Spend some time praying about what next steps you could and should take to strengthen your commitment to biblical community.

As you walk in community with the names listed above and you begin to confront, confess, repent, and forgive, together you will grow in your understanding of the cross of Christ. You see, the cross confronts our sin, causes confession, and delivers forgiveness. The cross is where unity is made possible and where biblical community can truly grow. Mission is but an overflow of living a cross-centered life, and living in biblical community is foundational to growing in the gospel.

An everyday missionary is committed to making disciples who make disciples.

INTENTIONAL
DISCIPLESHIP

Our role as everyday missionaries is to introduce people to Christ, actively be part of their journey to become like Christ, and teach them to repeat the process with others. The simple calling is to make disciples. A disciple is one who continually seeks to follow Jesus through the power of the Holy Spirit and in biblical community.

When I (Dustin) was a college freshman, I debated whether to go full force into the party scene or maybe take my walk with Jesus more seriously. I spent my first week on an A/B schedule—and I'm not talking about my academic schedule. On Thursday I spent my evening at a campus ministry singing songs to Jesus, while on Friday I was at a rush party trying to flee from temptation with five hundred of my new closest friends. It was a legitimate debate and I wasn't sure what I wanted to do, but it was my first year of "freedom" and the choice was all mine.

One Friday night one of the ministries was having a free cookout. Free food . . . I was there. While there I met Matt New, who was a year ahead of me in school. Matt and eight other guys and I hit it off and began hanging out: we ate wings, played ultimate Frisbee, went to football games, and read the Bible. That last part was a big deal, because the extent of my Bible reading had been on game days in high school, hoping that would get me on God's good side and clinch a football victory out of it. But with Matt and the crew, I found myself enthralled with what the Scriptures said. I wasn't just reading it as a

good luck charm; I was reading it because I wanted clarity and reason. Also, Matt walked me through the confusing passages and helped me find the answers in God's Word to my problems. I still remember Matt saying, "How do we interpret Scripture? With Scripture."

We'd get together to talk about what we read that week and then Matt would ask me great questions and then listen well. There wasn't a set time that we would we meet and there wasn't a set of ten questions he asked me every time. It was natural and just happened, as we would hang out here and there. For the first time I was growing in my relationship with Jesus. As I read the book of John, I discovered that the idea of discipleship was not a class or program I attended on a Sunday night, but rather a relationship with regular intentionality focused on the gospel and my spiritual growth. After hanging out with Matt for about two years, it finally hit me: I was being discipled.

I told Matt, "Hey, man, you're discipling me."

"Yeah, I know."

I acted as if I were offended. "But you didn't tell me."

His response was priceless and forever changed me. In his matter-of-fact manner, he said, "Well, now you know, and you should probably go do the same thing with some other guys."

I've been doing that ever since. And it all started with a guy who was just a year older than me, being willing to be an active part of my journey to become like Christ.

We are to make disciples who multiply themselves: disciples who make disciples.

JESUS' PROMISE AND INSTRUCTION

While on earth, Jesus offered some clear explanation about His role and ours in His kingdom. One was through a promise, and the other was through an instruction.

Earlier we talked about Jesus' promise in Matthew 16:18: "I also say to you that you are Peter, and on this rock I will build My church, and the forces of Hades will not overpower it." This is an incredible promise: Jesus will build the church. Often as Christians we take on

the responsibility that Jesus said He would deliver on. Are we called to edify the church? Absolutely. But too often we try to build what *we* have defined the church to be: a narrowed view that includes the building we gather in on Sundays and the programs that exist within the brick and mortar of that building. Our time quickly becomes wrapped up in the next, greatest, and latest program, which makes us feel we are building the church. But that is God's role. We can bring people into a building, but we can't bring them into the family. Only the Holy Spirit does that.

Instead we need to focus on the instruction Jesus gave His disciples—and, ultimately, us. After His resurrection, Jesus told His disciples: "Go . . . and make disciples of all nations, baptizing them in the name of the Father and of the Son and of the Holy Spirit, teaching them to observe everything I have commanded you" (Matt. 28:19–20).

We aren't suggesting that programs are wrong or that we shouldn't have church buildings, but when our structures and programs short-circuit the simple, sometimes messy, command to make disciples, then we need to revisit the Bible and, perhaps, rethink what our churches are doing. Because as we understand both Jesus' promise and His instruction, we must conclude that *Jesus builds His church and we make disciples.*

What practical implication does Matthew 28:16–20 have in your life right now?

YOUR MISSION: MAKE DISCIPLES

The life of the church and the mission of the church are inexorably bound within the all-encompassing reality of discipleship. Growth and discipleship cannot happen apart from Christian community, and your church's mission to make disciples can only be truly accomplished in the context of a community centered on the gospel. There are no "professional Christians" or "disciple-making specialists" who do all the work.

Anyone in need of sanctification (everyone) must submit to

discipleship under Christ within the context of biblical community, and anyone submitted to discipleship under Christ will obediently apply their gifts and personality to make disciples of friends, family, neighbors, and coworkers. No exceptions.

As we've mentioned before, too often church members forfeit their given mission and leave the work to pastors and missions agencies. But that's really not their role. One of a pastor's primary responsibilities is to equip *God's people to do the work* of ministry (see Eph. 4:12). Maybe you question your talents and abilities to serve or speak. But when you offer them to God, He uses them through you. God is in the habit of taking the ordinary person and using him or her for His glory. God could use any means to communicate the hope that is offered through Jesus, yet He chooses to use ordinary people like you and me (see Acts 4:13). No degree, no specialized class, no certain church status are required to make disciples where God has placed you.

As followers of Jesus, we are everyday missionaries who understand we are sent, just as Jesus was sent. Being entrusted with the ministry of reconciliation, everyday missionaries see God's heart for those who do not know Him, and they realize that they were once in a place without hope.

The apostle Paul reminded Christ-followers of that truth when he wrote:

If anyone is in Christ, he is a new creation; old things have passed away, and look, new things have come. Everything is from God, who reconciled us to Himself through Christ and gave us the ministry of reconciliation: That is, in Christ, God was reconciling the world to Himself, not counting their trespasses against them, and He has committed the message of reconciliation to us. Therefore, we are ambassadors for Christ, certain that God is appealing through us. We plead on Christ's behalf, "Be reconciled to God." He made the One who did not know sin to be sin for us, so that we might become the righteousness of God in Him. (2 Cor. 5:17–21)

Take note of the order in which the above passage was written.

• In Christ we are a new creation.
• Through Christ alone, we are made right before a Holy God.
• As new creations who are made right before God we now represent Christ to the world around us.

The above pattern of events is displayed similarly throughout Scripture. Earlier in chapter 6 of this book we worked through Isaiah 6 and we asked you to pay particular attention to the order of the events:

• Isaiah recognized God's holiness.
• Isaiah saw his need to be made right after realizing his sinfulness.
• God alone cleansed him of his sin and changed him.
• After being transformed, Isaiah committed to joining God in His mission.

And just as we are continually transformed by Christ's shaping us in biblical community, we continually seek for others to be reconciled to God and transformed just as we are—this is disciple-making. The church's mission is, in many ways, an expression of gratitude, and it's certainly (according to 2 Corinthians 5) a sign that we have life.

As we grow in our understanding that "He made the One who did not know sin to be sin for us, so that we might become the righteousness of God in Him," our hearts become compelled toward making disciples. We need to hear the simple truth of that Scripture often. That this glorious reality never becomes less true is enough to wreck us every day for the rest of our lives. That's what Jesus does: He comes in and wrecks our lives, in the best way possible. And when we are truly moved by something—when we genuinely love something—we can't help but talk about it.

This is why we cannot simply hope disciple-making into existence. We cannot put a sign on our church property that says, "Now Making

Disciples! Join Us." It takes time and effort and sacrifice. It's messy. Author Walter A. Henrichsen wrote, "Disciples are made, not born."[1] In other words, it's not easy. But it is doable.

Jesus was a great model for disciple-making. His ministry strategy was to pick twelve people and spend a ton of time with them. He didn't give them a manual or send them to a conference; He just did life with them. For three years they traveled, ate meals, and did ministry together. And then after the crucifixion and resurrection, Jesus stood before them and told them to keep doing what He taught them, and that He would be with them (see Matt. 28).

And they did. Empowered by the Holy Spirit, the gospel spread from twelve men to millions upon millions of people for the next two thousand years. What started as an intense three-year flame of life-on-life discipleship turned into a forest fire of epic proportions.

YOU REPRODUCE WHO YOU ARE

My (Dustin's) father was a carpenter. As early as I can remember, if I saw him driving a nail, I found some crew member's hammer and did my best to mimic him. From childhood on, we replicate what we see our parents do. This carries forward into school age as we are influenced by friends and peer pressure. We are continually shaped one way or another by our environments, especially the people around us. We are a fiercely relational people.

Think about it: Odds are at some point you've heard a parent, teacher, or coach say, "Do as I say, not as I do!" And when you hear that statement, you naturally push back because you realize that isn't how things work.

Wayne Cordeiro, pastor of New Hope Community Church in Oahu, Hawaii, told a group of pastors, "You teach people what you know, but you reproduce who you are."

I (Dustin) sought to make this statement a personal mantra as I led my church. For instance, one of my greatest joys as a pastor was doing "Family Vacation" with our church. Once a year we would take a retreat with all of our members and reflect on God's work, study the

Scriptures together, talk about where God was taking us, and do whatever we could to have fun. In the effort to have "fun" on one particular trip, we decided to organize a dodge ball tournament. We broke into teams in an elimination-style tournament, which we played in a parking garage. The theory being, if you can dodge a parking garage pillar, you can dodge a ball! (Did I mention I was a very young pastor?) My team was eliminated early, so I watched our church family compete against one another. There was so much pride-filled smack talk, it was crazy. One girl threw the ball while she simultaneously hit her hand on a pillar (there was blood) and then proceeded to tell the college guy across the way to get his tail out of the game.

Scenes like this continued throughout the tournament and toward the end I leaned over to my wife and said, "What is wrong with these people? They want to win way more than they care for the people they're playing the game with."

In only a way my wife can, she replied, "Hmmm, you teach people what you know, but you reproduce who you are." If you can't say amen, say ouch, right?

My wife was right. I'd taught our church what it meant to love one another, what it meant to put one another's needs above the other, and what it looked like to fight against pride. And yet our church took a lot of their cues not from my teaching but from my life. I'm competitive to the point that I try to beat the driving destination time on my phone's GPS. That night turned into a time of personal confession and a move toward a repentant heart. I was teaching one thing but I was reproducing who I was.

If you want the people around you to live on mission, then you live on mission. If you want to see the people around you walk in humility, seek to walk in humility.

Discipleship is far more than just divulging information. Discipleship happens as we watch people and imitate them and as others watch us and imitate us. As the apostle Paul told believers: "Imitate me, as I also imitate Christ" (1 Cor. 11:1). Just as we have been served by following those who are more mature, we have the great task of

helping those behind us take the next steps toward a deeper relationship with Jesus.

Like a line of hikers ascending a mountain, we keep our eyes on those ahead of us to follow in their footsteps. We listen to the advice they throw back to avoid missing the next step. And as we do so, we also look over our shoulders to those behind us. We tell them what to watch out for, where the sure steps are. We reach back and pull them along when necessary, trying our best to make sure they reach the mountaintop.

As we pursue God's mission, we have to focus on following those ahead of us, while at the same time helping those behind us stay on track. That includes:

- investing in relationships with those around us;
- teaching people to study and be obedient to Scripture;
- using "teachable moments" and showing how the gospel impacts all areas;
- being honest about failures, which clearly displays living under grace;
- seeing ministry as a way to "get people done" rather than using people to get ministry done.

THE WRONG MAN

Toni was a college student in my (Dustin's) church when she became a disciple of Christ. God rescued her from a painful past, and she quickly got connected to my church where she continued to grow.

Amazed by Jesus' work in her life, Toni wanted to spread that good news to others and be a part of making disciples. God specifically gave her a heart for the homeless, so she and some friends started walking through a downtown park, handing out food, and starting conversations with the homeless people she encountered.

One afternoon she saw a small Hispanic man in his late thirties. He was passed out, drunk, lying in a ditch, adjacent to the park. Toni felt led to get his attention, so she said, "Hey, wake up!"

And he did. He woke up and began talking to Toni and the others. He introduced himself as "Alex" and told them about his past, which included why he was drinking *rubbing* alcohol.

The next Sunday, Alex came to church with Toni and her friends. His personality quickly began to show, as he would laugh and say things like, "You guys catch the wrong man."

What started as a gospel-fueled walk in the park for Toni led to incredible things for Alex. Soon Alex came to know Jesus. Alex was baptized in the midst of the roaring cheers of his new church family. Over time Alex got a job, moved off the streets, joined a small group, and started to minister to the homeless, bringing others around our church family.

When we join God in His mission, nothing is insignificant. A short conversation or even a walk in the park can lead to disciple-making opportunities when the God of the universe is involved.

Which is easier—to be disciples or to make disciples? How do the two work together?

What are some barriers that hinder you from being a disciple who makes disciples? What do you need to say no to so that you can say yes to disciple-making?

What is God preparing you for? How does that play into His mission of reconciliation?

The Bible is God's story of using people who overcome great obstacles to accomplish His mission. What are some of the obstacles in your life?

MISSION PRACTICES

*Identify people who
need the gospel.*

IDENTIFY

Everyday missionaries don't just study, learn, and sit around all day reflecting on the gospel in a quiet room. They have an urgency to act—living out their faith in real life. In this section we transition from solid gospel foundations to strong mission practices.

In studying Scripture—in particular the life of Jesus and the ministry of Paul—we have discerned four clear-cut practices to help as you live on mission:

Identify people who need the gospel.
Invest in others as you share the gospel.
Invite people into disciple-making relationships.
Increase disciple-making by sending people to make more disciples.

As you study these practices, ask the Holy Spirit for wisdom and insight into how you can pursue them.

People who live on mission are always on the move toward others. They don't wait for the world to come to them, they seek and find the people who have needs. Jesus was one of these movers. In Mark 5, Jesus encountered a man possessed by demons, who was an outcast in his community and forced to live in a graveyard among a herd of pigs. The graveyard was across the Sea of Galilee where Jesus had been

doing ministry. Jesus knew the man was there and decided to visit him. Jesus had nothing to gain by going to this man. After all, the great crowds who were following His ministry were on the opposite side of the lake. But Jesus went to that one man whom society had written off. He had compassion on him and ultimately healed him.

Your life on mission will require that you "go to the other side" for people. The people who need your help are not necessarily going to show up on your doorstep, so you have to identify them where they are and move toward them.

I (Aaron) met Kevin when I signed up for a group fitness class when I lived in New York City. This particular class had some intense requirements: For three months, I had to attend the class six times a week and I agreed to a strict fifteen hundred-calorie-a-day diet. If I stuck to the plan, the meals and the class were free. I just had to give a video testimonial about it at the end of the three months.

I didn't much care for the grueling process or the packed schedule or the lack of cheesecake and pizza, but it did allow me to meet a lot of people I wouldn't normally hang around. One of those guys was Kevin. He was an actor/director and had experienced many ups and downs. As we hung out in the class he opened up about the emptiness he felt, and he ultimately admitted that the path he was on was leading nowhere fast. As I and others in our church ministered to him, he eventually placed his faith in Jesus.

The fact that Kevin came to Christ was a group effort. Kristen, a member of our church, invited my wife and me to participate in that fitness class. Many people in the church went to great measures to show love and care for Kevin. Freddy, one of our other pastors, spent hours counseling and working with him. The truth is that none of us would have met him if we had been sitting still.

KNOW YOUR NEIGHBOR

As followers of Jesus, our job is to identify people in our sphere of influence and share the gospel with them. Do you know your neighbors? Do you know their names, their stories, their background, and their

spiritual beliefs? A staggering 28 percent of Americans do not know a single one of their neighbors, while 29 percent know just "some" of their neighbors.[1] Essentially more than half of Americans honestly do not know their neighbors at all. In Mark 12:31, Jesus told us to "Love your neighbor as yourself." If we are called to love our neighbors, then without excuse, we must *know* our neighbors.

In some cases those people will be from the same cultural background as us. In many other cases the cultural context may be different and it will be up to us to establish some common ground so the message of the gospel is clear.

I (Dustin) live in the suburbs of Atlanta where barbeque restaurants, sweet tea, and church buildings seem as numerous as sand on a beach. However, the range of spiritual beliefs is exceptionally diverse. On our street alone, my wife and I are the only ones who believe Jesus is the only way to a relationship with God. Our neighbors are a collection of everything from atheists to Muslims. That may cause fear with some Christians, but my wife and I see it as a blessing that God has favored us with our immediate area of influence. And that influence started by simply identifying who our neighbors are.

Though the gospel has to be foundational in the way we connect with those around us, if we don't think through how we communicate then we run the risk of people not hearing the message. The apostle Paul said that his goal was to "become all things to all people, so that I may by every possible means save some" (1 Cor. 9:22). This doesn't mean that he became a cultural chameleon and just blended in to his surroundings. No, he found ways to communicate the central truth of the gospel to different audiences.

GOSPEL THREAD

By nature we are all self-absorbed. It's easy to become consumed by ourselves, only to think about how situations affect us, to make friends and pursue relationships based solely on what they have to offer us.

In Greek mythology we find a sobering example of what self-obsession leads to. The legend of Narcissus tells of a man who stumbled

upon a pool of water, and upon seeing his reflection, he fell in love with his image. So enamored with himself, he was unable to leave the beauty of his own reflection, and Narcissus eventually died by the pool.

Like Narcissus, sin causes us to have eyes only for ourselves and whatever fleeting pleasures we believe will satisfy us. At the heart of this self-obsession is a form of idolatry. We set ourselves up as idols by expecting people and situations in life to give us joy, meaning, and approval. Meanwhile, all around us are people in desperate need of the gospel who go unnoticed. Our self-absorption blinds us to them.

When we meditate on the gospel, however, we realize that in Jesus we've already been given everything we are searching for. He offers us all the satisfaction, purpose, and validation we could ever need. Jesus not only gave everything *for* us, He also gave everything *to* us.

There is an unimaginable amount of freedom in understanding this. If our souls are satisfied in Jesus, we can stop being self-absorbed and move beyond ourselves and into God's mission.

As we spiritually mature, the Holy Spirit will turn our gaze outward. We will begin to see with new eyes, to have an accurate perspective on the world around us. We will notice that God is at work everywhere. Our eyes will see the needs we encounter every day and the people who are desperate for Jesus. Instead of wanting to *take* from others, we will want to *give* the hope we have.

In which areas do you tend to be self-absorbed? In what ways do you need the gospel to free you from self-absorption?

Pray and ask the Holy Spirit to reveal to you where He is already at work around you and how you can join Him. Write down anything He reveals.

GETTING PRACTICAL

So where do you join God in His work? The short answer is to start where you already are. Go where you already go. Just go with new eyes.

What do you do in life? Do you work? Your workplace is likely a

great mission field where God is already at work. Do you go to school? People on your campus need the hope of Jesus.

In Acts 17:26–27, we learn that God has placed us in distinctive places at exact times so that those around us may come to know Him.

"From one man He has made every nationality to live over the whole earth and has determined their appointed times and the boundaries of where they live. He did this so they might seek God, and perhaps they might reach out and find Him, though He is not far from each one of us."

What about your community? What about your city? Are there neighborhood meetings you can attend, sports teams you can coach, or other rhythms you can be part of to get to know those around you? What about your hobbies or interests? Where do your gifts and passions lie? What makes your heart beat faster? What do you look forward to? Perhaps all are things God will use to connect you with others.

COMPASSION, CONVERSATION, AND COFFEE

Smitty worked for a small local real estate company. The company's offices were only a few miles from his house, and most of his coworkers were already Christians. Smitty wanted to live out God's mission, but it seemed his normal rhythms didn't place him around others who didn't know Jesus.

There were two things Smitty enjoyed immensely: coffee and sleep. The coffee shop Smitty liked the most was on the opposite side of town and, considering traffic, going there would mean waking up an hour earlier than desired. In this circumstance, sleep won over the favorite coffee shop. That jaunt would not become part of Smitty's normal rhythm.

One morning Smitty overslept and was running late for work, and to make matters worse, when he got into his car, he noticed he was low on gas. He couldn't chance running out of gas so he stopped at Stu's to fill up. Stu's was an old, run-down gas station where you couldn't even pay at the pump. This meant Smitty would have to go inside and interact with an actual *human*.

Since Smitty had overslept, he hadn't made his morning cup of coffee. As he hurried into Stu's store, he smelled the heavenly aroma of

freshly brewed coffee. Smitty paid for his gas and asked the older lady behind the counter, Miss Helen, how much the coffee cost.

"Honey, the coffee is not for sale. I brew it fresh every morning for myself, but I'll pour you a cup if you'd like."

"Nah, that's okay, I'm good," Smitty said, though deep down he really wanted that cup of coffee. But Miss Helen insisted. Smitty glanced at his watch. He was already going to be late, so he accepted. As he watched her pour the coffee, he asked the simple question, "So how are you doing?"

"I'm doing okay," she said in a quieter voice. "Not great, but okay." The tone of her voice gave away the pain she was experiencing. And Smitty recognized that this woman needed someone to ask a few questions and offer a little time to listen.

God used that moment on a Wednesday morning when Smitty was low on gas and late to the office to help him identify the person God wanted him to eventually share the gospel with. The truth is, Smitty stopped at that gas station a few times every month. This was a normal rhythm for him. It's amazing what can take place when gospel intentionality is woven into the fabric of our everyday rhythms.

Start with whatever your natural rhythms are, because it's not by mistake where God has placed you. Maybe for you it isn't as much about where you are as it is *who* you are—how God has distinctly wired you. Maybe you enjoy biking, fishing, knitting, hockey, or painting. Whatever your passions and interests, they can often help you identify the people God is moving you to share the gospel and your life on mission with.

When we combine our natural rhythms or passions with the gospel and use them to build relationships, powerful things can happen. Our passions or placement (where we live, where we go) can help us identify opportunities for sharing the gospel.

List the people or groups you interact with in your normal rhythm of life. What on your list could be an opportunity for mission?

What are your specific passions and gifts? What opportunities for mission could lie there?

THE ECONOMY OF JESUS

To identify where God is at work, look first at the glaring needs around you. These may be physical needs among the poor, or maybe you live near a high concentration of single mothers or at-risk youth. On the other hand, needs may be more relational or spiritual than physical—people struggling with loneliness, depression, addictions, or even the hopelessness of greed and materialism.

A good rule of thumb is: Look in the margins of your world. Who are the people others tend to shy away from or avoid? Who are the "untouchables"? This doesn't have to be a homeless person asking for loose change. It's just as likely to be a person who struggles socially at work or school and who doesn't have many friends. Often being an everyday missionary requires stepping out and over social boundaries, looking for opportunities to identify the marginalized as you seek to put the gospel on display. Consider how Jesus identified the lonely and the marginalized people of His day.

- Jesus had an in-depth conversation at a well with a promiscuous woman who had been married multiple times and who was currently living in an adulterous situation. This woman had been ostracized by her community (see John 4:1–42).
- Jesus had supper at the house of a tax collector—someone completely despised (see Matt. 9:9).
- Jesus touched a leper no one would even think about getting close to (see Mark 1:40–45).
- Jesus protected a woman from being stoned to death who had just been caught in bed with a man not her husband (see John 8:2–11).
- Jesus identified ordinary, unschooled men as the ones he would pour his life into during his three years of earthly ministry (see Acts 4:13).

Jesus' economy is different from the world's economy. In the world, people are all about ascending—doing whatever they can to step up whatever ladder they are interested in. It's all about getting something they don't have.

Jesus' social economy is completely the opposite. It's about descending, not ascending. It's not about looking to see what you can get from others, but identifying how you can give to others. It's about pressing out toward the margins—to the people who need love and friendship.

Which people around you are marginalized or avoided by others?

What social boundaries could you step over to be a witness to the social economy of Jesus?

IDENTIFYING THE NEEDS THROUGH PRAYER

A central part of identifying people and their needs is through prayer. Ultimately we want to identify those whom God wants us to identify. If you want to know whom God is specifically calling you to love and care for, ask Him.

Pastor Charles Spurgeon was often asked about the secret to his church's success (Metropolitan Tabernacle in London, England). The church was seeing record numbers of people come to Christ and was known as one of the largest churches in the world (during the 1800s). Christians and young pastors would visit the church to try to figure out this amazing feat. When they came, surprisingly Spurgeon would not take the visiting leaders into the two-tiered grand sanctuary but rather to the basement. There the leaders found people praying for God's direction and His grace for the work of His church.

This was the secret to their success, or as Spurgeon called it, the "powerhouse of the church."[2] The powerhouse of a great move of God starts with prayer. The fuel of our mission is prayer. One of the best activities you can do as an everyday missionary is to walk or ride through your neighborhood and ask God to show you what He sees.

Ask God to help you identify the people and needs that you can help meet. Why not even stop reading this book now and pray before moving on?

IDENTIFYING THE NEEDS WITH OPEN EYES

Josh and his roommates were in their early twenties, living in a neighborhood where they were all part of the same church. After hearing a sermon about being on mission in daily life, they were convicted to look for opportunities for mission work in their context. But what could they do? They felt overwhelmed, not knowing where to start.

After praying, Josh had the idea that they should bake a bunch of cookies and deliver them to their neighbors and introduce themselves. Yes, a bunch of twentysomething guys baking.

One Thursday evening, after they successfully baked and stuffed baggies with cookies, the fellas started their trek. They introduced themselves to more than forty neighbors and overall received a warm reception. Afterward, they went home and discussed what they'd learned. They were amazed at how clear their direction was moving forward.

> Identifying who God is leading you to may be as simple as taking a short walk with your eyes open.

Simply put: Their eyes were opened to a massive need. Out of the forty or so homes they visited, almost half were single mothers raising children. And what do single mothers often need? A break.

It was such a simple, commonsense idea that the guys were blown away by how easily they saw the need after they opened their eyes and took a short walk.

Identifying who God is leading you to may be as simple as taking a short walk with your eyes open. Of course, it might involve much more than that, and God could lead you to a place farther from home physically or culturally. But no matter where He leads, it all starts with prayer and opening your eyes.

What are some practical things you can do to identify the needs around you?

List three different groups of people (neighbors, coworkers, etc.) you feel God is leading you toward with the gospel.

Stop now and ask God to reveal to you who He is burdening you for. After praying, write down the group or individuals He reveals.

Invest your life in others as you share the gospel.

INVEST

After identifying where God is at work around you, the next step is to take action and invest in those to whom God has led you. Paul made this part of the missionary process clear when he wrote to the church in Thessalonica: "We cared so much for you that we were pleased to share with you not only the gospel of God but also our own lives, because you had become dear to us" (1 Thess. 2:8). Paul is making the declaration that, of course, we must speak the gospel to those we identify, but we must also invest our lives—our time, our resources, our gifts.

So what did investing look like for Smitty and Josh, the two stories from the previous chapter?

For Smitty, it was an incredibly simple process:

1. Go to Miss Helen's gas station on the way to work every morning to get a cup of coffee.
2. Ask her how she is doing.
3. Pray for her.

Smitty discovered a lot about Miss Helen over the next several months as he stopped every morning for a cup of coffee and conversation. He would stand (no seats in the place) and listen as she talked about her four sons and all the grandchildren she was having to raise. Smitty was able to identify story after story of heartache and would say a simple prayer for her and be on his way. Smitty was able to display

compassion and grace to this woman and eventually to her family, but it all began with identifying the opportunity on a morning when he was running late.

Investing turned out to be simple for Josh and his roommates as well—it simply took time, energy, and the willingness to do a little yard work. Josh and his roommates devised a plan to serve the obvious abundance of single mothers raising children in their neighborhood. After praying and talking, they decided that by cutting grass and taking care of the yards of these mothers' homes, they could begin to build relationships with both the mothers and their kids.

So they began doing just that. A couple of times a month they gathered lawn tools (they had to borrow some from friends at their church—"poor college students" after all) and worked on as many yards as they could on that given weekend.

From there on occasion some of the girls from their church would offer free babysitting, so the moms could have a break and a night out without kids, a rare occasion for any mom, but especially single moms. The girls would play games, help with homework, and share a Bible story with a related craft. They realized they didn't have to wait for a magical vacation Bible school week in the summer to share the Bible with those kids. All of these modest investments led to great relationships with the mothers and their kids. If these moms needed anything, they knew a group of college guys and girls were willing and ready to help.

> Jesus not only modeled sacrifice through His death but also through His life.

Both Smitty and Josh understand that those who have been made right with God through Jesus will disadvantage themselves for the advantage of others.

GOSPEL THREAD

The gospel tells us that Jesus sacrificed everything for us. He laid down His very life as a ransom for many, not to be served but to serve (see

Mark 10:45). Jesus not only modeled sacrifice through His death but also through His life. Over and over throughout the Gospels, we see that while Jesus consistently poured His life into the people closest to Him, He sacrificially served all those whom His life intersected.

Mark 6:56 illustrates how Jesus' reputation to help those who were hurting and to meet their needs preceded Him: "Wherever He would go, into villages, towns, or the country, they laid the sick in the marketplaces and begged Him that they might touch just the tassel of His robe. And everyone who touched it was made well." And in Luke 6, we even see Jesus, on the Sabbath, stop in the middle of His teaching to heal a man whose hand was paralyzed. Jesus' heart for serving others was rooted in compassion—He sympathetically entered into another person's sorrow and pain. Another example shows that as Jesus traveled with His disciples He arrived upon a crowd and His first reaction, as recorded in Matthew 9, was to have compassion for them, because they were weary and worn out. Interestingly enough right after that, Jesus told His disciples that humanity was in great need and to pray that the Lord would send out compassionate servants to meet the needs of the world (see Matt. 9:37–38).

We live in places that are full of pain, whether we can see it tangibly or not. The homeless person is in great discomfort because of the cold and his tangible need for shelter, while the wealthy CEO in the gated community searches endlessly for worth and value. Their conditions are completely different but nonetheless both need someone to forsake passivity and have compassion for them. Sacrificially investing in others is anchored in the ability to have a care for them that drowns out our own ability to focus on self. And when believers join as a community and together invest their lives in those around them, they reflect Jesus in a more powerful way than they could ever imagine.

How is your view of mission and investing in the lives of others motivated by the gospel or something else? How is your view of mission influenced by the grace that Jesus has shown you?

INTENTIONALITY AS A WAY OF LIFE

If you are familiar with church activities, the first thing you think of when you hear the word *mission* might be a mission trip or an offering. While those things are certainly valid aspects of being a biblical community, they are, by definition, short-term with limited involvement. Being on mission is not always about going to a specific place—it's about being intentional where you are. That's investment. And investment is always intentional. It's a lifestyle choice.

> Being on mission is not always about going to a specific place—it's about being intentional where you are.

A missional lifestyle is rooted in the knowledge that God is already on mission around you, and He has placed you in your environment because He wants to use you to reach the people around you. It's a mistake to think that you will be intentional as soon as you move somewhere different or take the next step—if you're not on mission where you are now, you won't be on mission where you're going.

The great thing about intentionality as a way of life is that it goes where you go. If God calls you to move, you will already know how to be on mission to anyone around you. Your location may change, but your intentionality won't.

In what ways are your normal, everyday surroundings your mission field?

How can you grow to be more intentionally on mission where you are?

GETTING PRACTICAL

Once you've identified where God is at work around you and noticed opportunities for spreading the gospel, it's time to put intentional effort in investing into the lives of those people. In other words: Share your life with people. Make friends. Ask them to lunch. Throw a party.

Have a cookout. Invite them bowling. In short, build relationships.

As modeled by Jesus, another great way to build relationships is through serving. Learn the needs of the person or group and how you can help fill that need. If you were to get on a plane and fly to Rwanda, you would quickly discover the need for clean water. Identifying this need would move you toward figuring out how to dig wells and provide sanitary water. It's similar for your people: what are the "wells" that need to be built within your community and how do you build those "wells"? Remember Josh and the guys serving the single moms? They saw a "well" that needed to be built in the form of yards that needed to be cut. Their venture was a big investment, but the reward came through the relationships they and the girls from their church formed with the moms and their kids.

> Whatever you have to do—do whatever it takes to invest in the lives of others.

Of course fulfilling a need doesn't always have to be as big as a year-round neighborhood lawn service and free child care. It can be as simple as offering to help a neighbor make a one-time home repair. Whatever you have to do—do whatever it takes to invest in the lives of others.

Why wouldn't you just tell them about the gospel and move on? Because, while there is certainly room for telling someone you barely know about Jesus (see Rom. 10:14–15), it often works best to build a relationship with them first. (We'll talk more about this in the next chapter.) In general, people don't like to feel they are a project, or that they are receiving a sales pitch, and they may have the wrong idea about why you want so badly for them to become a follower of Jesus.

Just like any friendship, as a relationship grows deeper, you will naturally get to the things that are important. If Jesus is important to you, then as your relationship grows He will naturally come up in conversation.

INVESTING: BOTH/AND

The methods you use to intentionally invest in relationships may differ depending on the person and situation.

Some situations will look like a somewhat normal friendship because the person you're investing in is fairly similar to you culturally. He or she may be a coworker with whom you share common interests, such as golf. In other situations, though, God calls us to cross significant cultural barriers. Investing in these scenarios may require a concerted effort since it might be difficult to discover common ground. It's not either/or—it's both/and.

For example, Paul and Jennifer felt a strong call to be missionaries to the Hispanic community in their city. This direction reoriented their lives in many ways. They learned Spanish. They looked for like-minded believers to join them, and they even moved into a predominantly Hispanic neighborhood.

Depending on where God has you and whom He has led you to identify, your methods of investment may look different from those of other people pursuing the same missionary process, and that's okay. The important thing is that we are all joining God in His mission to seek and save the lost.

A HELPFUL TIP

If you're having trouble figuring out how to invest in those around you, try this simple tool: Ask people how you can pray for them. When you're building relationship with neighbors, coworkers, or friends, simply say, "Hey, this may seem weird to you, but I'm a Christian so I pray for people. Is there anything I can pray for you about?"

Even non-Christians will oftentimes gladly accept prayer and respond to this question with genuine things that are going on in their lives. Many times this question leads to great conversations and a deeper relationship.

A Christian couple moved to a new neighborhood and after meeting some of the neighbors they eventually asked that question: "Is there anything we can pray for you about?" Late one night several

weeks later, they heard a frantic knock at their door. Upon opening the door, they saw a distraught young woman on their porch weeping. The young woman's first words were, "Are you guys the ones who pray for people?"

If you're stuck, try this and see if God doesn't use it to lead you to just the people you're supposed to invest in.

RELATIONAL EVANGELISM

This act of investing in relationships to spread the gospel is called *relational evangelism*. The reason it works well is because we are more likely to listen to and trust something a friend tells us than something a complete stranger communicates to us. It is much more powerful when we share the gospel with people with whom we also share our lives. We see Jesus do this very thing with His disciples—taking time to invest on a deep level. They spent an extraordinary amount of time together, and church history reveals that it was time well spent.

> The Great Commission calls us not simply to make converts but to make disciples.

The Great Commission calls us not simply to make converts but to make disciples. So as we invest in people's lives, we help them continue to take the next step toward Jesus (refer back to chapter 8), with the hope that one day they will become a reproducing everyday missionary as well. (We will dig deeper into this concept in chapter 12.)

How often do you spend quality time with people who don't know Jesus?

Look back at your answers from the "Identify" questions. What would it look like for you to invest in the people God has helped you identify?

Whom could you invite to come alongside you to invest in the community and people you identified?

WELL WORTH IT

Guess what Josh and his friends discovered early on in their efforts? Seriously investing in the lives of others takes a lot of time and energy.

> Seriously investing in the lives of others takes a lot of time and energy.

They had to learn to sharpen a mower blade. They had to edge many corners and turns of sidewalks, and rake leaves in the autumn as they watched more leaves falling where they'd just raked. They had to sacrifice other things in their schedules and show up ready to work, even during times they'd selfishly rather be doing something else.

But do you know what else they discovered? All of their sacrificial investments were worth it. They got to see the look of relief on the faces of those moms. They got a chance to talk about Jesus when asked over and over, "Why are you doing this and not charging me?" They got to witness and hear about the bonds that the kids formed with the girls over the months, asking their moms when the girls were coming over again. Did all the moms come to Christ and begin serving all the other single moms in one instantaneous swoop? No, but the gospel was made clear both through words and their selfless serving.

Investing our lives isn't easy and often we may wonder why we don't see a return on our investment. Yes, we want to see transformation, but remember we are moved toward compassion because we have been shown much compassion. Give it time. Be patient. Pray a lot and allow God to work in His timing. Remember that ultimately our mission is to actively display the gospel while offering the opportunity to be saved by Jesus, but God is the only one who can ultimately transform a heart.

What would you have to give up or sacrifice in order to tangibly communicate Jesus to those whom you have been able to identify?

List three tangible ways you can invest your life in those people you have identified.

Invite people into disciple-making relationships.

INVITE

Jesus was all about the invite. Jesus invited people to eat with Him, surrender to Him, give up their possessions, walk with Him, follow Him, be healed, rest, and the list goes on. Jesus was not even above inviting Himself over for dinner either. In Luke 19, we learn that Jesus entered Jericho and started to teach. The crowd was overwhelming, pushing and shoving, trying to hear and see Jesus. To get a better vantage point, a man named Zacchaeus climbed a tree nearby. Zacchaeus was a rich tax collector who not only collected taxes but essentially cheated people out of money, so the people hated him. As Jesus worked His way through the people, He stopped and singled out Zacchaeus, asking him to get down from the tree. What Jesus did next not only shocked the on-looking crowd but also the most hated man on the block, Zacchaeus. Jesus invited Himself to be a guest at the tax collector's house. The invitation went beyond just hanging out and maybe sharing a meal together; Jesus essentially invited the man to leave his life of lies and possessions to experience salvation. A man who was hated as a result of his sin experienced an unmerited love and acceptance that he had never felt before.

This is Jesus' invitation to our world. Jesus concludes His time with Zacchaeus by clearly and concisely stating His mission: "The Son of Man has come to seek and to save the lost" (Luke 19:10).

God Himself is on a rescue mission as He invites people into right relationship with Him. Joining God in His mission will require that we become willing to extend the invitation to others.

GOSPEL THREAD

Ephesians 2:11–22 beautifully expounds upon the fact that Jesus has reconciled us to God through the cross and made us into one family, or one household, with God. The passage starts off by reminding us of what God has carried us from and then moves on to explain what He has delivered us to. Verse 12 states: "At that time you were without the Messiah, excluded from the citizenship of Israel, and foreigners to the covenants of the promise, without hope and without God in the world." So why do we remember? Because we didn't always have the hope we presently have in Jesus. Once we were orphans outside the family of God. We were desperate and hopeless in our sin.

The gospel calls us to remember this fact because, as we once were, many others still are separated from God. Many hopeless spiritual orphans are still lost in their sin and need to be invited into God's family. Remember what it was like to be on the outside, and that remembrance will strengthen your desire to see those on the outside brought in.

But we don't present the gospel to them and once they accept it, leave them there. Instead we invite people into a deeper, discipling relationship with God. As Paul stated, "We proclaim Him, warning and teaching everyone with all wisdom, so that we may present everyone mature in Christ" (Col. 1:28).

Who has made a major investment in your spiritual growth? How have they helped you become more like Christ?

INVITING: BOTH/AND

Just as methods of investing in relationships may look different depending on the situation, the same is true for methods of inviting. Inviting people into discipling relationships will look different in different contexts.

Think back to Paul and Jennifer's story in chapter 10. They moved to a Hispanic community and began to invest their lives in the people

there. They invited other like-minded people from their church to join them in the mission and, while no one else actually moved there, they did get some help.

Slowly but surely, Paul and Jennifer began to see results. Several people became willing to explore Jesus with them, so they invited them into their home where they explored Christianity. Two of them eventually came to know Jesus, an incredible experience, but Paul and Jennifer soon realized something: They were unsure of what to do next. Because there wasn't a nearby church that contextually fit the Hispanic neighborhood, they began their own Bible study, where they answered questions, worshiped, prayed, and encouraged one another toward spiritual growth. In other words, they made disciples.

They soon discovered that pursuing these disciple-making relationships eventually led to genuine biblical community among the new believers. They became a family. And in the midst of this happening, the disciple-making environment provided a context for more people to meet Jesus, because people invited their friends and relatives, who were skeptical about Jesus, to come and investigate Him. Paul and Jennifer had no idea that something so beautiful could happen in a community they never would have placed themselves in without the Spirit's prompting. For Paul and Jennifer, the disciple-making relationships created biblical community where it formerly didn't exist. And as they learned, the universal principle here is strong: As we invite people into disciple-making relationships, biblical community is formed.

> As we invite people into disciple-making relationships, biblical community is formed.

For Patrick, the invitation looked different from Paul and Jennifer's experience. For years Patrick led a small group of men and noticed that the group was growing spiritually stale. So he prayed and decided that they needed to use their community as a tool for mission.

Several of the men enjoyed playing disc golf, so once a month, instead of having their usual small-group meeting, they played disc golf and invited friends they were investing in to join them.

Steve, one of the men's coworkers, played a few times. Steve enjoyed hanging out with them, and eventually he figured out that they met at other times during the month as well. Even though he wasn't a Christian, he expressed interest in hanging out during their small group time. During the meetings he was amazed by the way the men treated one another like family. They fought for, supported, and even confronted one another in love when necessary. Steve observed the men modeling Jesus' words: "By this all people will know that you are My disciples, if you have love for one another" (John 13:35).

After a few months of hanging out with the guys every week, Steve became a believer in Jesus. Not long after, he started to invite some of his other friends who didn't know Jesus to hang out with the group. One by one, several of his friends also came into the group and eventually a number of them took next steps toward Jesus.

The last thing we want this to sound like is an infomercial for mission with the idea, "If you follow this ninety-day plan of *Life on Mission*, you too will see everyone you know come to Christ." Of course it doesn't work that way. But biblically speaking, this process can lead to great possibilities among your friends and in your community. Try it and plead for the Holy Spirit to work in the hearts of those you have identified and are investing in.

> As we invite people into biblical community, disciples are made.

For Patrick, the small group leader, the biblical community that already existed formed the perfect environment for disciple-making relationships. As we invite people into biblical community, disciples are made. Again, it's not one or the other; it's both/and. Like a two-headed coin, the results should be the same either way you flip it.

MAN ON A HILL VERSUS CITY ON A HILL

Make a concerted effort to be on mission in community with others. Too often the road of evangelism and mission is one people attempt to travel alone. But we need the encouragement, support, and account-

ability of community as we live on mission.

In Matthew 5, in what has been termed the "Sermon on the Mount," Jesus gave great metaphors for what mission could and should look like. One of the specific ideas was comparing the idea of our mission and message to light.

You are the light of the world. A city situated on a hill cannot be hidden. No one lights a lamp and puts it under a basket, but rather on a lampstand, and it gives light for all who are in the house. In the same way, let your light shine before men, so that they may see your good works and give glory to your Father in heaven. (Matt. 5:14–16)

One of the keys to understanding this passage is to recognize that Jesus was addressing a community of people, and He illustrated the carrier of this great hope as a city.

There has never been a city that had a population of one. One person on a hill does not qualify as a city no matter how hard he or she may try. A city is a city because it has a large number of people who make up its population. We are called to invite people into biblical community so they can experience the "city"—the family of God.

People need to see the grace of God lived out among a group of people. They need to see other believers repenting, confessing, rejoicing in God's grace, and forgiving others. They need to see the gospel applied to life. People desperately desire to belong to something bigger than themselves, and despite being more connected than ever (social media), many people are incredibly lonely.

You are not meant simply to show off the light that you have as an individual, but rather you are meant to display the light of the gospel through a community of people who are unified in Jesus. Biblical community is like a city on a hill that emits a great light to those who are wandering around in a dark, desolate desert.

GETTING PRACTICAL

If you are like Paul and Jennifer, pressing out on mission into the fringes where biblical community is not readily available, you need to have a laser focus on discipleship. Invite those you are investing in to meet with you as often as possible and pour into them. Invite them to study the Bible with you or in a small group environment, teach them the basics of the faith, and talk about the gospel continually, showing them how it applies to their lives.

Within the North American church, evangelism is too often reduced to inviting someone to a church service in hopes that the preacher's message that day is engaging, states all the right ideas, and in the end leads to your friend walking an aisle, filling out a response card, or raising her hand. Please understand us clearly, there is nothing wrong with investing for the sake of inviting a person to a church service, but know that seeing someone move closer to Jesus is going to take much more than that. If we are going to reach people where they are, we have to be bold enough to speak the gospel where they are and not wait on the "professional" to do what every believer has been explicitly called to do.

When reading Romans 10, for many of us, we have the tendency to get excited about verse 13—"Everyone who calls on the name of the Lord will be saved"—and verse 15 (NIV)—"How beautiful are the feet of those who preach good news." Both verses communicate amazing truth and are without question something that we should celebrate. Unfortunately, I (Dustin) believe one of the most unapplied and overlooked verses in the Bible is sandwiched between verses 13 and 15: "But how can they call on Him they have not believed in? And how can they believe without hearing about Him?" (verse 14).

The good news of God's grace cannot be mimed; it must be spoken. Other than one's own salvation there may not be a greater joy than explaining the gospel and watching God do what only He can do: save people.

INVITING PEOPLE TO JESUS

We've talked extensively about the gospel, but before moving forward we want to give a clear way to explain the gospel in conversation and invite someone to surrender his or her life to Jesus.

The Starting Point: Brokenness

As you invite someone to Jesus, you need to start with something they can relate to. We live in a broken world, surrounded by broken lives, broken relationships, and broken systems. This brokenness is also seen in the poverty, hunger, violence, crime, pain, suffering, and death around us. Everyone has experienced or witnessed this brokenness and everyone has at one point or another tried to find a way to make sense of that reality. Even the most stoic of characters has tried to put the pieces of life together. This is a perfect place to begin your invitation. You can say something as simple as, "Have you ever thought about the reality of how broken our world is? Do you ever see or experience this in your own life?"

God's Design

When people endeavor to make sense of life, their attempts often end up being an exercise in futility and ultimately lead to more brokenness. Many will say, "I believe that everyone is on their own path." But they know deep down their path too often goes nowhere. It is at this point you could begin to talk about God's perfect design for humanity. God originally designed a world that worked perfectly. Creating a man and woman, God placed them in a world where everything and everyone fit together in harmony. He wanted them, and you, to worship Him and walk with Him. Originally, things were the way they were supposed to be. So what happened to God's perfect world?

Wanting to be in charge, humans rejected God and His original design. The Bible calls this sin. Like a virus, sin is passed down from generation to generation, distorting the original design. The consequence of sin is brokenness and separation from God.

Gospel

At this point we need some good news. Because of His love, God did not leave us in our brokenness. Jesus, God in human flesh, came to us and lived perfectly according to God's good design. Jesus also came to rescue us—to do for us what we could not do for ourselves. This is the good news—this is the gospel.

Jesus took our sin and shame to the cross, dying to pay the penalty of our separation. Jesus was then raised from the dead. His death and resurrection provide the only way for us to be rescued from our brokenness and restored to a relationship with God. Jesus wants to rescue us by His life.

Invitation

Simply hearing this good news isn't enough. We must repent of our sinful brokenness and stop trusting in ourselves. We must put all of our trust in Christ's death on the cross and resurrection from the dead.

This is when you could ask if they want to trust Jesus. I (Dustin) will never forget going to lunch with a classmate, Travis, my senior year of college. Travis wanted to talk about some frustrations he was dealing with and he heard I would be someone good to talk with. In the middle of his monologue about the disaster his life had become (a sign of brokenness), I stopped him and said, "Hey, man, you need Jesus. It's as simple as that, and you need to become a Christian *right now.*"

I'd never been that bold just to interrupt someone in midsentence and invite them to follow Jesus, but I felt the Holy Spirit prompt it and so I acted.

What happened next blew my mind. Travis said, "You're right!" He then dropped his head and started praying. He told God his sin in great detail—right there over a rack of ribs and corn on the cob.

To be fair, I've had similar conversations since then and most of the people didn't give their lives to Jesus. But the point is simple: When God prompts, speak the gospel.

They may or may not accept, but you've done what God asked you to do: offer the invitation. In whatever way you can, be intentional

about helping people take steps toward Jesus. Continually ask yourself (and the Holy Spirit in prayer):

• What can I do to help this person take the next step toward Jesus?
• How can I serve them and encourage growth?
• What do they need to hear or learn?

Share yourself with people so they can see how you handle situations and apply the gospel to your life. Allowing people to see that you do not have it all together will give way for them to see God's grace applied in your life. Too often, as Christians, we see it as our duty to present ourselves as having it all together, nice and neat. When we live this way, we do not give an opportunity for people to see God's grace at work in us and to grasp that following Jesus is possible for them too.

Humbly and openly repent of your sin to testify that your righteousness is in Jesus and model that Christians are not perfect, but covered in grace. Apologize when necessary and don't let yourself become a puffed up, prideful, "super Christian" who is above doing anything wrong. Remember: You can teach people what you know, but you are going to reproduce who you are.

Is your life highly visible to those you are discipling? Are they able to see you grow, repent, and change?

What steps can you take to be more intentional with those you are raising up?

How can you foster biblical community with those you are discipling?

If you're like Patrick, investing in people whom you can invite directly into your biblical community, you are set up to use your existing community as an instrument for discipleship. Talk to your community

about being on mission together. Cast the vision of being a city on a hill that you invite others to join. Have a discussion about the people in whom your group is investing. How can you invite them to become part of your community? Are any of them interested enough in Jesus to want to come to your group meeting? If so, invite them.

Some people might not be interested in taking that step yet (or might be uncomfortable being around people who pray and talk about the Bible), but there are other great ways to invite them into relationship. One way is to establish relational rhythms for your group, such as planning a weekly "nonthreatening" activity that a skeptic would be interested in participating in and that would still build community. For example, your group could grab lunch together every Wednesday. The options are endless—you can turn anything your group enjoys doing into an opportunity to invite others into relationship.

Name a person(s) you have been investing in who you could invite into your biblical community.

Who is in your life who needs to hear the gospel message? What's stopping you from sharing?

How can you cultivate an environment in your community that accepts new ideas and people?

What rhythms could your church establish to serve as relational avenues to invite others to join?

*Increase disciple-making
by sending people out.*

INCREASE

The goal of the mission is not just to have an awesome church, small group, or discipleship group. It's not to keep only the same people around you forever because you like doing life with them and ministering to them. It's not to selfishly keep what you have.

The goal is to see a movement! To see the gospel spread, new people come to know Jesus, and new disciples made. It's to see more people groups reached, more small groups launched, and more churches started in order to enfold the lonely into biblical community. Spreading, sending, and multiplying movements—these are the goals for the good of people and the glory of God.

MULTIPLICATION IS THE HEART OF A MOVEMENT

A simple way to see a movement of new believers is to raise up the new disciples in strong biblical foundations and to send them out to repeat the missionary process of identifying, investing, inviting, and increasing. The previous statement is not a job description for a pastor but rather the intent given to every believer of the gospel.

The most effective thing you can do for the mission is to reproduce yourself as many times as possible, so that there are more everyday missionaries out in the world speaking and displaying the gospel of Jesus.

Jesus testified to this truth in Matthew 28:18–20 when He gave His disciples the Great Commission: "Then Jesus came near and said to them, 'All authority has been given to Me in heaven and on earth. Go,

therefore, and make disciples of all nations, baptizing them in the name of the Father and of the Son and of the Holy Spirit, teaching them to observe everything I have commanded you. And remember, I am with you always, to the end of the age.' "

He mentioned it again in Luke 10:1–3 when He sent out seventy missionaries in pairs to testify about Him: "After this, the Lord appointed 70 others, and He sent them ahead of Him in pairs to every town and place where He Himself was about to go. He told them: 'The harvest is abundant, but the workers are few. Therefore, pray to the Lord of the harvest to send out workers into His harvest. Now go; I'm sending you out like lambs among wolves.' "

The harvest truly is abundant—we showed this at length in chapter 2. Millions upon millions all around us desperately need Jesus. Together, we must pray for God to send out workers, with the understanding that we become part of God's answer to those prayers.

GOSPEL THREAD

As you follow the timeline from Jesus to the early church and throughout history, you can trace the path of disciple-making all the way to your own life. Think about it: Jesus poured Himself into His disciples, the disciples raised up others in the faith, they sent out others—and so on until the chain eventually got to you. How crazy is that? You are part of a huge family tree of discipleship and mission that reaches all the way back to Jesus Himself. If you actually take a moment to reflect on that, it really is miraculous.

> That kind of gospel reflection will make you want to give away what you have instead of grasping tightly to it.

And what an honor to think that your life on mission continues that gospel thread into the future. That kind of gospel reflection will make you want to give away what you have instead of grasping tightly to it. That's why even though you may want them to remain in your small group, church, or city, you'll eventually grow to a place where you'll have a great desire to see people reached for

the gospel, and you'll grasp that you are part of making that desire a reality. Love for Jesus and His mission will compel you to discover the leaders around you, develop them in the gospel, and deploy them to reach more people with the good news.

How does the gospel motivate you to continue that "gospel thread" into the future?

SPREADING AND SENDING

Think back to Paul and Jennifer, the couple who wanted to reach a Hispanic community in their city. As their small group continued meeting, several new people came into the group and eventually became believers. The first believers were growing and showing a lot of spiritual fruit and maturity. So Paul and Jennifer began to pray about how they could equip them to spread the gospel, and even began to ask questions about it while teaching through the whole idea of discipleship.

One man, Alberto, had many friends who lived across town. He told Paul and Jennifer that God had burdened him for that group of people. They talked about it, and all agreed that God was calling Alberto to start a similar ministry in that neighborhood. So with the group's support, training, and accountability, Alberto made plans to move there and repeat the process that Paul and Jennifer had started years before. This man had been so changed by the gospel that he carried a God-given desire to see another community transformed by that same gospel.

What about Patrick's group—the man who intentionally used disc golf as a means toward pursuing God's mission with his small group? What did "increase" look like for him?

Steve, the new Christian in his group, had already quickly become a missionary, growing in maturity and inviting other men into the group who eventually became believers. So Patrick intentionally equipped and developed Steve, as well as a few of the other men. In essence he followed the apostle Paul's model, in which he told his

disciple Timothy: "What you have heard from me in the presence of many witnesses, commit to faithful men who will be able to teach others also" (2 Tim. 2:2). Within Paul's one statement he lists three generations of disciples: Paul (first generation), Timothy (second generation), and the person Timothy will "commit" to (third generation).

Patrick, our disc golf guy, understanding the 2 Timothy 2:2 principle, and seeing how large his group had grown, sent out a few men to lead new groups of their own—to reproduce what they had seen happen in their group. So Patrick cast a vision for their group to multiply. He taught them that God had made room for them when they were without hope (Eph. 2:11–22), so the gospel should compel them to do the same for others. The men caught the vision, and even though they were close friends and wanted to keep the group they had formed, they all gathered to pray over Steve and the other men, knowing that sending them out was what God wanted.

Look at where you are and ask the Holy Spirit if He may be sending you out of your comfort zone for His sake.

GETTING PRACTICAL

The practical step of increase is all about starting the process again by sending people to identify, invest, and invite their friends and family into new communities. Keep in mind that this will not happen overnight and will require prayer and patience as God matures your community.

As you spend time with those you are discipling, you'll want to begin asking them: "Who are you called and able to reach that I can't or won't reach?" For example, let's say you are a forty-year-old man who grew up playing hockey and there is a professional ballet dancer in your group. Guess whom she is likely to reach that you may not?

You got it—ballet dancers.

Maybe a guy in your group has a background in inner-city gangs. Don't you think that because of his history, he has an incredible opportunity at reaching that community?

Besides common interest or backgrounds, there's an even simpler level to consider: The people you are discipling know a lot of people

you don't know. And of course, since they already know them, they are more likely to reach those people than you are.

Regardless of specifics, being intentional about increasing is just that—being intentional about increasing. It's raising up others and then strategically sending them out to do what you have done for them.

The goal is to train them so well that you could disappear and the ministry would not skip a beat. Let this question guide your disciple-making:

How can you raise up those you are pouring yourself into to take over and do for others what you did for them?

Intentionality in increasing the number of people living on mission is central to seeing the kingdom impacted. This will not happen by itself, and we need to equip and develop people as much as possible.

As far as helping grow and mature those around us, here is a simple illustration that many ministries and organizations use.

- *I do; you watch.* In this stage, you are leading and they are simply being led and discipled.
- *I do; you help.* You see enough growth and desire in them to want to begin equipping them for leadership. You still lead, but you start to let them help however they can. You let them lead Bible studies, mission activities, or discussions.
- *You do; I help.* In this stage, you give them more ownership. You let them lead more consistently while still helping and keeping them accountable, correcting them when necessary.
- *You do; I watch.* This is the stage in which you fully trust them to lead on their own, but they need a little more practice. So you give them the reins as much as possible to lead while you still participate and watch them.
- *You do; someone else watches.* This is where the disciples are actually sent out to lead on their own. They are now the leader and someone else is watching them.

From here, the process is repeated with someone else. And then the person they raise up does it somewhere else . . . and that person they raise up does the same thing elsewhere . . . and . . . you get the point.

This is how a movement is accomplished: by intentionally developing everyday missionaries, sending them out to reach others by the power of the Holy Spirit.

JOINING DAD AT WORK

As we look at the daunting reality of our current state in North America and pressure that comes with being an everyday missionary, we must have a healthy perspective on what joining God in His mission really looks like.

Growing up, I (Dustin) spent a lot of time around construction sites. While I loved all the machinery and the thrill of watching the building process, mostly I wanted to be there because I got to be with my father. My dad was a master carpenter who was well respected among those in and around our community. His attention to detail was bar none and his drive to get the job done right was remarkable. In time I became a "glorified gofer," which meant I retrieved whatever the crew needed (nails, level, 2x4s, water, etc.). I didn't mind that so much, but really I hoped for the opportunity to have my own hammer and join the crew.

I'll never forget the day when I was around twelve years old and my dad brought together the whole construction crew and presented me with my first hammer. He announced that I was now part of the actual crew. I felt like I'd just been knighted, southern style.

"Well, don't just stand there," my dad said. "Get to work." Everyone laughed, and I knelt on the floor to start nailing down the sub-flooring—the base before you install the finely finished floors—as all the other crew stood back to watch this kid take his first official "I'm on the crew" swing of the hammer.

I aligned the nail and took a swing.

Missed. I bruised the floor.

Second swing, contact. But the contact I was hoping to be the nail

was intercepted by my thumb. Now my thumb was pulsating and quickly turning blue. And my face was quickly turning red.

My third swing bent the nail. Now I found myself tapping on both sides of the nail in an effort to straighten the "S"-shaped nailed I had just created. By this point I was so nervous, I wanted to walk off the job.

But then my dad came over and covered my small hand with his large hand.

"We can do this, son."

And next thing I knew, *bam-bam-bam*—the first nail was down. *Bam-bam-bam.* The second nail was down. Nail after nail was going down.

I thought, *Check me out, fellas. I'm a carpenter. It just took me a minute. No big deal. I'm a natural.* And then I feel the pressure of my dad's hand still on top of mine. He was doing the work; he was doing the heavy lifting. He was making it happen.

"We can do this," he told me again.

God speaks a similar idea to us even now. It is His mission. It is His work, and God Himself extends to us the great invitation of getting to go to work with our Dad.

Think about the people you've invited into discipling relationships. Whom are they equipped to reach that you aren't? How can you help them identify people around them who need the gospel?

Whom do you need to raise up and send out? How can you practically develop him or her to be an effective missionary to do for others what you've done for them?

In what ways can you celebrate and support groups you send to reach those who are lost and without the gospel?

MINISTRY STEPS

An everyday missionary has a plan of action, understanding there will be the battle of pitfalls throughout the journey.

PITFALLS AND PLANS

The goal of this book is to equip you biblically and practically for living out God's mission. We believe as you dig deeper into the gospel and live out this mission, ministry will begin to take place. Pastors, church leaders, and ordinary you and me: We're *all* in this mission together.

Ministry is simply the overflow of the gospel of Jesus in you working itself out into practical terms in the world around you. Being grounded with a strong gospel foundation, paired with the formation that occurs as you join God in His mission, leads to a ministry that allows you to effectively relate to the people in your community. In other words: Effective ministry is the result of a solid gospel foundation and clear understanding of the mission of God. While the gospel and mission of God never change, your ministry practice may look different depending on your immediate surroundings. Inevitably God uses different ministry practices to strengthen your understanding of the gospel as well as the mission you have been given.

In light of this goal, we want to end the book with some reflection questions to help you put everything you have learned together and formulate a ministry plan of action. However, pursuing a life on mission is not without pitfalls, so before we press into making an action plan, we'd like to address some of those pitfalls. Ask the Holy Spirit and your community to help you guard against any of these you may be susceptible to.

PITFALL #1: MISPLACED PRIORITIES

A fairly historical struggle for people who are living on mission is to get their priorities out of order. Many times an unhealthy pace of ministry can lead to burnout and even to the destruction of a family. We can be so blinded by the never-ending needs that we can neglect our more important responsibilities.

As mentioned previously, in the mid-2000s my wife and I (Dustin), along with a few other people, planted a church in downtown Columbia, South Carolina. The first year was incredibly rough. Our attendance was only a few dozen, and most of those were college students, so our offerings were around twelve dollars and a bag of Skittles. In year two we began to see some incredible traction. We were baptizing people, working closely with our city, moving homeless people off the streets, seeing marriages restored, and were rapidly running out of space. I was twenty-seven years old and working overtime alongside some of my best friends to make this mission work. I was preaching numerous times each Sunday, launching what felt like five new small groups a week, interacting with the local news outlets in regard to our involvement with the homeless, and we had hired a couple of staff. Seeing people grasp and live out the gospel was amazing.

Then on a Sunday in November 2007, I stepped off our porch on my way to our church's evening service, where I was set to preach to the overflowing crowd.

"See you there!" I told my wife.

"No, I'm not coming tonight," she said.

What? Her words stopped me mid-step.

"I probably won't be back," she continued. "I don't much like our church." Then she began to cry. "I'm glad this mission is going well, but I don't have any community myself, my relationship with Jesus is dry, and the church we started is *not* helping either one of those."

My response? I thought, *Don't you know I have a sermon to preach? And here you are crying? What are you doing?*

And then God hit me with His own question, *No, Dustin. What are you doing?*

Mission is great, but sacrificing your family on the altar of mission is not what God has called us to. The good news is that God changed my priorities that day and my wife didn't leave the church I pastored, but fell deeply in love with the ministry we had been given there. That moment was a wake-up call, which began a journey that I'm still on, in which I'm learning what it means to actively love my family more than I love the high of doing ministry.

The greatest mission effort you will ever participate in is the one that involves the people who sit around your dinner table at night. As you pursue the mission God has for you, never let that truth grow cold to your heart.

Andy Stanley has a great book called *When Work and Family Collide*, in which he says that when faced with a decision to cheat either your ministry or cheat your family—always choose to cheat your ministry.[1] Why? Ministry will always be there and will never be finished—not to mention the fact that God is in charge of it and other people can do it. Your family, however, is a different story. Who beyond yourself is called to love and take care of them? Exactly. No one. Your family is a responsibility given uniquely to you by God, and you are called to make that responsibility a priority. If you don't pursue being on mission *with* your family then the mission you seek is a failure before you even begin.

Please avoid this pitfall at all costs. Love your family more than you love your ministry. If you get this backwards, you are not a faithful missionary no matter what kind of ministry fruit you see.

PITFALL #2: REFUSING TO REST

Because we tend to equate busyness with success, many people living on mission get so caught up in the duties of ministry, work, school, and family that they never take the time to rest. Think about it. How often do you hear people say how busy they are and how they're doing their best to keep it together? It's almost as if getting no rest because of a long to-do list is a sign of success. But here's the truth: Busyness is *not* a badge of honor to wear.

In Genesis 2, God instituted a day of rest, not as a rule to keep us

> **Busyness is not a badge of honor to wear.**

from achieving everything we want but for the purpose of our own health. It is a gift for us, and refusing to receive it is detrimental to our health and to our mission. Without rest, we will eventually burn out physically, emotionally, and spiritually. Our lives will be negatively affected, including the people nearest and dearest to us. It won't be a pretty sight.

I (Aaron) am not a very regimented guy. I tend to be a hard-charger, and taking time to rest can be especially hard for me. In fact, I just spent time with a professional life coach who told me that my energy level ranked near the top of the almost three million people who had used the assessment tool he took me through. His counsel to me served as an affirmation, but also as a warning: I need to take time to rest.

The idea of a balanced life is a myth to me. What I mean is that there are seasons when we have to work really hard, and finding the perfect amount of time to rest in the midst of that may be difficult. However, life has its rhythms. So if we find ourselves running really hard for a season, we need the next season to include significant times to rest.

The way this plays out for me is that my job may require my travel schedule to be heavy for a few weeks. When that is the case I have to be intentional that the following several weeks keep me at home. I may even take a couple of vacation days so I can spend significantly more time with my family.

One last practical example—because most of the people I work with are located all over North America—is that I spend a significant amount of time on my iPhone. I could literally return phone calls and emails 24/7 if I chose to. When it was time for our last family vacation, I decided to leave my phone at home. That break was amazing. I spent focused time with my family, free from the potential worries that email and phone calls can bring. Here is what I also discovered: The world can exist without me being electronically connected to it all of the time.

Working 24/7 and refusing to rest is a telltale sign of works-based theology. The Sabbath reminds us that we are approved, based on Jesus' performance and not our own, and many of us need to apply the gospel to this part of our lives. As you aggressively seek to live on mission, please

be careful to trust God with this area and take the time to rest in Him.

PITFALL #3: WEIGHT-OF-THE-WORLD MENTALITY

Another pitfall is when we attempt to carry the weight of the world on our shoulders. Some people think they are the only ones who can carry out a specific type of ministry. They think they are the *only* people who can reach so-and-so. This stems from the belief that their mission will no doubt fall apart without them leading every facet.

When Carmen and I (Aaron) decided to get involved in foster care/adoption in New York City, it was hard not to take on the weight of the world. We found out quickly that thousands of foster kids needed care and a home. Something in us made us wonder if we were doing enough by only taking two children. Of course, we knew that it was not practically possible to do more than we were doing, but we still fought a sense of guilt wondering if we could do more.

We are indeed called into meaningful ministry, but we are not responsible for every aspect of it. We are not supposed to carry 100 percent of the weight. We must move to a place where we understand who truly carries the weight and actively believe the truth of God's responsibility in this whole mission. As Paul said in 1 Corinthians 3:6–7, "I planted, Apollos watered, but God gave the growth. So then neither the one who plants nor the one who waters is anything, but only God who gives the growth." We work and we toil, but God gives the growth.

This is incredibly freeing, as it takes away an enormous amount of pressure and also teaches us that we can empower others to do the work of ministry and rebuke the lie that we should do it all on our own. Pray earnestly that God will give you the discernment and reasoning to know when to say yes, when to say no, and when to say not now.

PITFALL #4: LONE-RANGER MENTALITY

The lone-ranger mentality is dangerous because it leads us to unhealthy isolation. Referring to chapter 7 on biblical community, we see that no one is intended to be on mission alone. We need not only

the support of community, but also the ability of others to see our blind spots. No one can see his own blind spots, hence the word *blind*.

We have to remember that the church is a body and that each part is expected to carry its own weight in conjunction with the whole. No one part is expected to do everything. In one of my opening stories I (Aaron) talked about how I felt overwhelmed in New York City. I wondered how I was going to make a difference in that vast metropolis. Essentially, I felt defeated because I could not do enough by myself. After a while, I realized that God was calling many people to live on mission and that was how God was going to accomplish His purposes. It was not all dependent on me!

When we seek the mission in and of ourselves we forfeit the idea of the kingdom. We were not called to live out the mission of God alone, and we reflect the kingdom of God when we work with other believers. Together we are better suited to carry out God's mission.

PITFALL #5: MINISTRY IDOLATRY

Any good thing that has turned into an ultimate thing is dangerous, and this can definitely be true of living on mission. It is easy for our ministry motive to turn from being about Jesus to being about personal success. I (Dustin) had a friend who discovered that mission was not just what he did during a summer trip once a year but that his own neighborhood was his year-round "mission trip." I remember he called it his "life trip." It was incredible to watch as God opened his eyes to what it looked like to identify, invest, invite, and increase those who lived right around him. I was so encouraged as I watched God work through and in him. The guy was growing by leaps and bounds, but gradually he began to change. I noticed that all he talked about was, "My neighbor *this* . . . my neighbor *that*" and there didn't seem to be much else going on.

You may think, *What's wrong with that?* But if his neighbors were responding to his efforts to serve them, then he would say, "It was an incredible week." If they weren't responding, then he would say, "This week could not be any worse."

My friend was putting his hope in whether the people were

responding to his efforts or not. At that point his mission had become his "giver of life." Mission will never give you life—only the God of the mission can do that.

> If you don't pursue being on mission **with** your family then the mission you seek is a failure before you even begin.

I (Aaron) can "outdo" Dustin when it comes to his church-offering story. Dustin mentioned earlier in this chapter about receiving an offering that was twelve dollars and a bag of Skittles. Well, the second offering we collected at our church in NYC was six dollars and a gum wrapper (seriously). I will never forget how defeated that made me feel. I went home that night and wanted to cry. After a while, I reflected on why that offering made me feel the way it did. What I realized was that my personal success was tied up on the "success" of the church. I felt that the offering was a reflection of my abilities.

At the end of the day it is natural for a person to want his or her ministry to go well, but what if things *don't* go so well? What if the ministry God calls you to turns out to be difficult and messy and you never see positive results? What if, like Moses, you find yourself wandering in the desert with stubborn people who won't listen to you? If your motive is success in ministry, your joy will quickly dry up. Too often we pursue ministry with our true goal not as pure faithfulness but the fruit we hope to see. Ministry fruit is a great thing, but fruit as motive is fruitless.

The solution to this, of course, is that success in ministry cannot compare to the hope we already have in the privilege of knowing God and will not fulfill us even if we achieve it. God is the true reward, and we get Him no matter what. If we really grasp that on a heart level, then our joy and contentment are secure no matter the outcome of our ministry efforts—because relationship with God never changes. Our deepest affections are designed to be tied to our Creator, not the visible fruits of Him working through us.

We are called to be faithful and trust God with the results. This relieves a lot of pressure and allows ministry fruit to be a thing we celebrate, but not the ultimate goal.

Which of these pitfalls will you need to be on guard against as you pursue life on mission?

PUTTING IT ALL TOGETHER

Can you imagine if millions of Christians in North America came to understand and live out the ideas expressed in this book? What if scores of believers woke to the reality that their lives on mission really do matter and began to live as the everyday missionaries they are called by God to be?

Our schools, workplaces, and neighborhoods would suddenly be captured with hope. Light would invade the darkness in innumerable ways as Christians find an eternal and weighty purpose for their lives.

Needs would be met. Disciples would be made. The lonely would be enfolded into community. The hope of Christ would be tangibly and verbally expressed. Single moms would be taken care of, orphans would be adopted, the broken would find healing, and addicts would be set free. The course of our continent would change forever by a simple idea applied to real, ordinary, everyday life.

This renewal both could be and should be, and it's certainly what we're praying for. But you don't determine what happens to the world—you determine what happens in your own life. You and you alone will decide if these ideas have any impact on your life, or if you'll simply go back to business as usual.

So . . . what's next for you?

Well, that depends on . . . you. But we hope that you will do two things:

1. Grow in the gospel and biblical foundations. We hope you will meditate on the gospel and seek to continually apply it to every fabric of your life. We hope you will pursue maturity, community, and discipleship as lifetime principles.

2. Actively pursue the missionary practices. We hope that the foundations you pursue will compel you toward a biblically

faithful missionary effort. We hope you will identify, invest, invite, and increase.

We believe this book will serve as a helpful tool in your development as a missionary, and we pray that you will consult it often and use it wisely. As you grow in the gospel and the biblical foundations for ministry, you will by grace become the everyday missionary God is calling you to be as you faithfully live your *life on mission*.

So . . . really . . . what's next for you?

QUESTIONS TO SET YOUR PLAN OF ACTION

What has the Holy Spirit prompted you to glean from this book?

What steps do you need to take in order to grow as a missionary?

How can you grow to be more grounded in the missionary foundations (the gospel, spiritual maturity, biblical community, intentional discipleship)?

Very practically, what can you do to pursue the missionary practices in the next three months?

IDENTIFY: Whom has God led you to identify as people who need the gospel?

INVEST: In what ways can you invest your life in those people while you share the gospel?

INVITE: How can you invite them into disciple-making relationships?

INCREASE: In what ways can you send them out to make new disciples?

LEADER'S GUIDE: SIX-WEEK STUDY

HOW TO USE THIS LEADER'S GUIDE

Life on Mission seeks to deliver a solid gospel foundation with everyday mission practices. It offers engaging stories threaded with powerful questions to help people take their next steps to living life on mission.

Ideally, we encourage the reader to discuss and process the content within community. Our goal is for small groups, missional communities, Sunday school classes, church plant core teams, and church staffs to work through the book together and allow it to shape the way they live on mission.

This Leader's Guide is intended to be a helpful resource for any leader or group facilitator. It is based on a six-week discussion of the book (taking a few chapters per week). However, feel free to take this at your own pace and spread the discussion over more weeks if that would be better for your community.

The guide is simple and straightforward, including highlights from each chapter to help focus your conversation, a few helpful questions to guide discussion, and some practical challenges. You may want to read the chapter highlights aloud as a refresher before starting each chapter's discussion. Also, refer back to the questions embedded in the content of each chapter. Your group members should have already worked through those questions during their reading for that designated week.

SIX-WEEK READING PLAN: OVERVIEW

WEEK 1: THE BIG PICTURE (CHAPTERS 1 & 2)

Chapter 1: Everyday Missionary

CHAPTER HIGHLIGHTS:
- Your life has a mission. If you are a follower of Jesus, then He has a purpose and plan for you.

- An everyday missionary is one who lives life on mission where God has placed him or her.

- The ultimate aim of our lives is to glorify God!

- Understanding that God is sovereign is essential for mission. A missionary must recognize that God is at work in the world and ask His children to respond to that work.

- If you determine the success of mission, then that isn't a God-centered mission. If God directs the success of the mission, however, then you are on the right track.

- The reality of God's love and grace should propel us toward living on mission.

- A weak gospel foundation leads to fragile mission practices.

- The overall goal of all life on mission is to serve the glory of God. That goal in turn provides the necessary fuel and endurance for the mission.

DISCUSSION QUESTIONS:
1. How have you struggled with figuring out what God's will is for you? In what ways is it freeing to think that His primary will is for you to simply glorify Him where you are?

2. How do God's sovereignty and God's love form the correct motivation for mission? How do they take away unnecessary pressure from mission?

3. Which camp do you tend to fall in most?

   a. The "I'm not a professional" camp

   b. The "I'm too busy pondering" camp

   c. The "Why are we doing this?" camp

4. What from chapter 1 stood out to you, and how could this impact your life?

Chapter 2: The Current Reality

CHAPTER HIGHLIGHTS:
- America's evangelical population loses 2.6 million people per decade.

- While many evangelical denominations are on the rise, they still fall woefully behind in catching up with the population growth and cultural changes.

- Entire cities that were once vibrant, gospel-transformed places are now spiritually boarded-up wastelands.

- When things seem bleak and hopeless, God shows up and breathes life into our situation.

DISCUSSION QUESTIONS:
1. Did this chapter change your perspective about the need for the gospel in North America? If so, how?

2. How does understanding the realistic spiritual landscape in North America affect your thoughts toward your everyday life?

3. What from this chapter stood out to you, and how could this impact your life?

WEEK 1'S PRACTICAL CHALLENGE:

Ask God to let you see your community and city as He does.

Spend some time this week examining your city and community and ask God to show you where it lacks gospel influence. As God begins to reveal the current reality, ask Him how you can live on mission where you are.

WEEK 2: THE BIG PICTURE (CHAPTERS 3 & 4)

Chapter 3: The Mission of God

CHAPTER HIGHLIGHTS:

- As we push deeper into what it looks like to join God in His mission, we should take caution not to skip "why" it's important.

- The current reality of our world is certainly a motivation for what we do as everyday missionaries, but the ultimate motivator is God Himself.

- Our missionary God is not waiting for you or me—He is already at work.

- God has always been about forming a gospel people for a gospel mission.

- As we are changed and freed by Jesus, we are compelled to want to be where He is—right in the middle of the greatest rescue mission ever given, led by God Himself.

DISCUSSION QUESTIONS:
1. Discuss the practical challenge from the previous week. How did it go? What did God show you?

2. In what ways does understanding God's mission throughout history affect you?

3. How do you see your everyday life as a part of God's mission to bless the world? In what ways can this truth be something you are constantly aware of?

4. What from this chapter stood out to you, and how could this impact your life and ministry?

Chapter 4: Kingdom Realignment

CHAPTER HIGHLIGHTS:
- God is still King of His kingdom.

- Jesus is a King who gets down into the mess of humanity, who goes to ultimate lengths to seek and save the lost and restore people back into His kingdom.

- In the standard economy of a kingdom, kings are not servants and servants are not kings, yet King Jesus is both.

- Jesus calls us to repent of building our own kingdoms.

- The kingdom of God is the best thing we could ever get swept up in.

- He calls us to repent of chasing after our own fame and glory, and instead pursue His fame and glory. It's the best trade we could ever make.

DISCUSSION QUESTIONS:
1. How does knowing that God is our King strip away any hopelessness that might creep in when we consider the decline of the church in North America?

2. What self-centered kingdoms have you pursued with your time, energy, and resources? What do repentance and getting swept up in God's kingdom look like for you?

3. What from chapter 4 stood out to you, and how could this impact your life and ministry?

WEEK 2'S PRACTICAL CHALLENGE:
Walk around your neighborhood this week and introduce yourself to any neighbors you do not know. Bake some cookies (or something else delicious) and give them as gifts. Be bold. Have fun. Watch God work.

WEEK 3: GOSPEL FOUNDATIONS (CHAPTERS 5 & 6)

Chapter 5: The Gospel

CHAPTER HIGHLIGHTS
- Living out a gospel mission is not a guilt or fear-driven task—it is the good life.

- A missionary who isn't grounded in the good news of Jesus is no missionary at all because he or she does not have good news to proclaim.

- Though we are more sinful than we'll ever truly know, we are *still* loved by God more than we could ever imagine.

- If Jesus is your Savior, the pressure is off.

- The gospel is not based on what you do for God, but what God has done for you. It is not "you do" but "Jesus did."

- The gospel is how we become Christians, but it is also how we grow as believers—through meditating on God's Word and applying it to every fabric of our lives.

- The gospel stands opposed to earning, but it should by grace propel us toward great effort.

DISCUSSION QUESTIONS:

1. Discuss the practical challenge from the previous week. How did it go?

2. How do you struggle to believe that "if Jesus is your Savior, the pressure is off"?

3. In what ways do you tend to believe that God's feelings toward you rise and fall based on your spiritual performance (instead of being secured by Jesus' righteousness)?

4. What from chapter 5 stood out to you, and how could this impact your life and ministry?

Chapter 6: Spiritual Maturity

CHAPTER HIGHLIGHTS:

- As you grow a deeper understanding of your identity in Jesus and submit your sinful nature to the Holy Spirit's work, spiritual maturity will be consistently present.

- The gospel doesn't just free you; it changes you.

- Knowledge does not equal maturity.

- Our world does not need people who know more facts about God, but rather people who are falling deeper in love with God.

- Humility, obedience, and application are far more closely tied to maturity.

DISCUSSION QUESTIONS:

1. Where have you seen Jesus at work in your life recently? How is He growing you toward maturity?

2. Are there areas where you have knowledge but not application and obedience? Are there things you need to repent of in order to grow spiritually?

3. What fruit of the Spirit is less prevalent in your life?

4. What fruit of the Spirit is more prevalent in your life?

5. What from chapter 6 stood out to you, and how could this impact your life and ministry?

WEEK 3'S PRACTICAL CHALLENGE:

Contemplate the ways you try to earn God's love and write those ways down. Then pray each day that God would free you from the performance trap. Ask the Holy Spirit to reveal any areas that you haven't given over completely to Him and ask Him to show you what pursuing health and obedience in those areas looks like in a typical week. Once He shows you, commit to following that. (Example: If you've been convicted about your prayer life, commit to pray for fifteen minutes every day this week.)

WEEK 4: GOSPEL FOUNDATIONS (CHAPTERS 7 & 8)

Chapter 7: Biblical Community

CHAPTER HIGHLIGHTS:
- Biblical community is built on committed, authentic, and caring relationships that urge one another toward Jesus and His mission.

- Everyday missionaries understand their biblical calling to be anchored to a group of believers, to whom they confess, with whom they repent, celebrate, and live in faith.

- You can't choose Jesus and not choose the church. They are a package deal.

- Biblical community is the group of believers with whom we walk through the good, the bad, and the ugly while digging deeper together into the gospel.

- Community is essential because it is one of the primary ways we grow in the gospel.

- We need one another to carry out the mission of God.

DISCUSSION QUESTIONS:
1. Discuss the practical challenge from the previous week. How did it go?

2. With whom are you walking in biblical community?

3. When was the last time you confessed your sin to another believer?

4. What changes could you make to move more purposefully toward being in consistent biblical community?

5. What from chapter 7 stood out to you, and how could this impact your life?

Chapter 8: Intentional Discipleship

CHAPTER HIGHLIGHTS:
- As followers of Jesus, everyday missionaries understand they are sent, just as Jesus was sent.

- Jesus' ministry strategy was to pick twelve people and spend a ton of time with them.

- Disciple-making happens best in the context of relationships and biblical community.

- Discipleship cannot be divorced from community, because discipleship happens in community.

- As we pursue God's mission we have to focus on following those ahead of us, while at the same time helping those behind us stay on track.

DISCUSSION QUESTIONS:
1. Discuss the practical challenge from the previous week. How did it go?

2. Do you struggle with seeing mission as a "have to" rather than a "get to"? If so, what is off in your perspective?

3. Who has helped you take next steps toward Jesus? How can you encourage and thank them this week?

4. Who has God put in your life who you can intentionally help take next steps toward Jesus?

5. What barriers make it difficult for you to make disciples who make disciples? How can we as a group help remove those barriers?

6. What from chapter 8 stood out to you, and how could this impact your life and ministry?

WEEK 4'S PRACTICAL CHALLENGE:

1. Confess any current sin to another believer in your community, and ask them to remind you of the gospel in response.

2. Write down the name(s) of the person(s) you are going to help take their next steps toward Jesus and call them this week to set up a time to hang out.

WEEK 5: MISSION PRACTICES (CHAPTERS 9 & 10)

Chapter 9: Identify

CHAPTER HIGHLIGHTS:

- If our souls are satisfied in Jesus, we can turn our eyes away from ourselves. By grace we can stop being self-absorbed. Instead we will identify people who desperately need the hope of Jesus.

- Where do you start in your efforts to join God in His work and be a disciple-maker? The short answer is to start where you already are. Go where you already go. Just go with new eyes.

- When we combine our natural rhythms and passions with the gospel and use them to build relationships, powerful things can happen.

- Identifying who God is leading you to may be as simple as taking a short walk with your eyes open.

DISCUSSION QUESTIONS:

1. Discuss the practical challenge from the previous week. How did it go?

2. Who has God placed around you that He may be calling you to be on mission with (coworkers, neighbors, friends, those who share hobbies/interests, etc.)? Mention specific names and pray for them.

3. Are there ways your passions or natural life rhythms may focus God's mission for your life?

4. What group of people is God leading you to focus your mission efforts on?

5. What changes could you make to be more consistently aware of what God is doing around you?

6. What from chapter 9 stood out to you, and how could this impact your life and ministry?

Chapter 10: Invest

CHAPTER HIGHLIGHTS:

- Growing in the gospel will move you from identifying those around you who need the hope of Jesus to investing your life in theirs.

- As an everyday missionary, you are rooted in the knowledge that God is already on mission around you, and the fact that He has placed you in your environment because He wants to use you to reach the people around you.

- Being on mission is not about going to a specific place— it's about being intentional where you are.

- Share your life with people. Make friends. Ask them to lunch. Throw a party. Have a cookout. Invite them to go bowling. In short, build relationships.

- As we invest in the lives of people, we help them continue to take the next step toward Jesus, with the hope that one day they will become a reproducing everyday missionary as well.

DISCUSSION QUESTIONS:

1. Discuss the practical challenge from the previous week. How did it go?

2. What would it look like for you to invest in the people God has led you to identify? How can you consistently build relationships and spend time with them?

3. What changes might you need to make in order to truly invest in people?

4. What practical step can you take this week to invest relationally in someone?

5. What from chapter 10 stood out to you, and how could this impact your life and ministry?

WEEK 5'S PRACTICAL CHALLENGE:

Pray about who God wants you to be intentional with (neighbors, coworkers, friends, people with similar interests/hobbies, etc.). Write

down one to three specific names and pray for them every day this week. Then write out how you will give of your time and energy to invest in them. Then do it.

WEEK 6: MISSION PRACTICES AND MINISTRY STEPS (CHAPTERS 11, 12 & 13)

Chapter 11: Invite

CHAPTER HIGHLIGHTS:
- As we invite people into disciple-making relationships, biblical community is formed.

- Invitation includes making a concerted effort to be on mission in community with others.

- You need the encouragement, support, and accountability of community while you are on mission.

- Invite people to give their lives to Jesus. Speak the gospel.

- People need to see God's grace lived out among a group of people. They need to see other believers repenting, confessing, rejoicing in God's grace, and forgiving others. They need to see the gospel applied to life.

- Biblical community is like a city on a hill that emits a great light to those who are wandering around in a dark desert.

DISCUSSION QUESTIONS:
1. Discuss the practical challenge from the previous week. How did it go?

2. What would it look like practically for you to invite people into disciple-making relationships?

3. Do you have consistent relationships with other believers (biblical community) with whom you could invite others to join?

4. Who do you feel God is leading you to invite into a relationship with Jesus?

5. What conversation might you need to have with someone about the gospel?

6. What from chapter 11 stood out to you, and how could this impact your life and ministry?

Chapter 12: Increase

CHAPTER HIGHLIGHTS:
- Love for Jesus and His mission will compel you to identify the leaders around you, raise them up, and send them out to reach more people with the gospel.

- The goal is to see a movement! The movement includes spreading the gospel, bringing people into relationship with Jesus, and growing them to maturity. We desire to see more people groups reached, more churches started, and more small groups launched to enfold the lonely into community.

- The most effective thing you can do for the mission is to reproduce yourself as many times as possible, so that many more missionaries spread the good news of Jesus.

- The goal is to train them so well that you could disappear and the mission would not skip a beat.

DISCUSSION QUESTIONS:

1. Discuss the practical challenge from the previous week. How did it go?

2. What is the hardest part about making disciples and reproducing yourself as a missionary?

3. How does Jesus' promise in the Great Commission that "I am with you always, to the end of the age" (Matt. 28:20) encourage you in your disciple-making efforts?

4. What does the increase step look like in your setting? How can you be intentional about raising up others and sending them out?

5. Discuss the leadership development process from the end of the chapter. What would this look like in your context?

6. What from chapter 12 stood out to you, and how could this impact your life and ministry?

Chapter 13: Pitfalls and Plans

CHAPTER HIGHLIGHTS:
- Ministry is simply the overflow of the gospel in you working itself out into practical terms in the world around you.

- An everyday missionary has a plan of action, understanding there will be pitfalls throughout the journey.

- Many times an unhealthy pace of ministry can lead to burnout and even to the destruction of a family.

- Busyness is *not* a badge of honor to wear.

- We are called into meaningful ministry, but we are not responsible for every aspect of it.

- It is easy for our ministry motives to turn from being about Jesus to being about personal success.

- Actively pursue the missionary practices.

- Identify, invest, invite, and increase.

DISCUSSION QUESTIONS:

1. Of the five pitfalls mentioned, which one tends to be a problem area for you and why?

2. Discuss the first three personal reflection questions from chapter 13.

3. Summarize and discuss your action plans based on the missionary process you learned in this book. Which one is the easiest? The most difficult? Why?

4. How does what you have learned in *Life on Mission* impact your community/church/group, etc.?

WEEK 6'S PRACTICAL CHALLENGE:

1. Pick one person from your prayer list from Week 5 and intentionally invest in him or her (for instance, invite them to lunch, a dinner party, a local sporting event, a concert, or to coffee). Whatever you do, be sure to ask a lot of questions about their life and show genuine interest. Also, try to involve other Christians from your community.

Tip: During this step, a helpful question to ask people is: "This may sound weird to you, but I'm a Christian and like to pray for people, so is there anything I can pray about for you?"

Many times this simple step opens the door for more intentional conversation as you follow up with prayer requests.

2. Write down the person(s) from your group who need to start new groups of gospel influence and have a conversation with them about moving toward next steps.

3. Share your *Life on Mission* plan with the group and how you have begun the journey of an everyday missionary.

NOTES

Introduction

1. http://www.nyc.gov/html/dcp/html/census/pop_facts.shtml.
2. http://quickfacts.census.gov/qfd/states/28000.html.
3. Lyle Schaller, *44 Questions for Church Planters* (Nashville, TN: Abingdon Press, 1991), 14–26.
4. J. D. Payne, *From 35,000 to 15,000 Feet: Evangelicals in the United States and Canada: A State/Province, Metro, and County Glimpse* (jdpayne.org, 2010), 12.
5. Ibid., 12.
6. Ibid., 9.
7. Ibid. 10.
8. http://www.christianitytoday.com/ct/2012/may/quebec-prodigal-province.html?start=3. Also cited in http://en.outreach.ca/Resources/Research/tabid/5233/ArticleId/6938/Is-Canada-Becoming-a-Post-Christian-Country.aspx.
9. Tim Keller, "Why Plant Churches" (Redeemer Presbyterian Church, 2002), 6. http://sermons2.redeemer.com/sermons/why-plant-churches.
10. Ed Stetzer, *Planting New Churches in a Postmodern Age* (Nashville: Broadman & Holman, 2003), 10.
11. Jim Collins, *Good to Great* (New York, NY: HarperBusiness, 2001), 65.
12. http://www.nycreligion.info/?p=1165.
13. Matthew 16:18: [Jesus said to Peter,] "On this rock I will build My church, and the forces of Hades will not overpower it."

Chapter 1: Everyday Missionary

1. Psalm 46:10, ESV.
2. Exodus 34:14.
3. John Piper, *Let the Nations Be Glad* (Grand Rapids, MI: Baker Academic, 2001), 17.
4. "Westminster Larger Catechism" http://www.reformed.org/documents/index.html?mainframe=http://www.reformed.org/documents/larger1.html.

Chapter 2: The Current Reality

1. John Dickerson, *The Great Evangelical Recession* (Grand Rapids, MI: Baker Books, 2013), 26.

2. http://jacksonville.com/tu-online/stories/063008/lif_296770295.shtml.

3. http://www.pcaac.org/church-search/_Also cited in http://www.usnews.com/opinion/blogs/robert-schlesinger/2011/12/30/us-population-2012-nearly-313-million-people.

4. http://www.efccm.ca/pdfs/WelcomeToTheFamily.pdf.

5. http://www.cmacan.org/statistics.

6. *The Great Evangelical Recession*, 22.

7. http://www.usatoday.com/story/news/nation/2012/12/12/census-whites-us-2043/1763429/. Also cited in John S. Dickerson, *The Great Evangelical Recession*, 33.

8. http://www.reginaldbibby.com/images/Revision_Bibby_CSA_Presentation,_Ottawa_May_09.pdf.

9. http://www.slate.com/articles/life/faithbased/2012/11/re_evangelizing_new_england_how_church_planting_and_music_festivals_are.html.

10. Adam Miller, "Overview of Montreal," http://www.namb.net/montreal/overview/.

11. Ibid.

12. Ibid.

Chapter 3: The Mission of God

1. Genesis 1:26–27.

Chapter 4: Kingdom Realignment

1. Romans 8:28.

Chapter 5: The Gospel

1. Tim Chester, *You Can Change* (Wheaton, IL: Crossway Books, 2013), 15.

2. John Van Diest and Alton Gansky, *The Secrets God Kept* (Carol Stream, IL: Tyndale, 2005), 145.

3. Louie Giglio, in a message delivered at Send North America Conference, July 30, 2012.

4. Tim Keller, "Knowing that we know God," preached 11/13/1994, http://www.monergism.com/thethreshold/articles/onsite/jesusourdefense.html.

5. Dave Harvey, *When Sinners Say "I Do"* (Wapwallopen, PA: Shepherd Press, 2010), Kindle Edition.

Chapter 6: Spiritual Maturity

1. Ephesians 3:18, ESV.

2. Nehemiah 1:5, ESV.

3. Esther 4:14, ESV.

4. Bruce Ashford, ed., *Theology and Practice of Mission* (Nashville, TN: B&H Books, 2011),18.

5. This is a paraphrase of the language that Wayne Grudem uses in his *Systematic Theology.* Wayne Grudem, *Systematic Theology: An Introduction to Biblical Doctrine* (Grand Rapids, MI: Zondervan Publishing, 1994), 214, 337, et al.

6. John 3:16, ESV.

7. Dave Harvey, *When Sinners Say I Do,* Kindle Edition. This is not a specific quote but a theme from the book.

Chapter 8: Intentional Discipleship

1. Walter A. Henrichsen, *Disciples Are Made Not Born* (Colorado Springs, CO: David C Cook, 2002).

Chapter 9: Identify

1. http://www.pewinternet.org/2010/06/09/neighbors-online/.

2. Charles Spurgeon, edited by Robert Hall, *The Power of Prayer in a Believer's Life* (Lynnewood, WA: Emerald Books, 1993), 12.

Chapter 13: Pitfalls and Plans

1. Andy Stanley, *When Work and Family Collide* (Colorado Springs, CO: Multnomah Waterbrook, 2011).

ACKNOWLEDGMENTS

A book is the result of the ideas of countless people. Though two people were given the opportunity to write the book, it would be entirely appropriate to list hundreds of people on the cover who have contributed to its fruition.

In 2010, the North American Mission Board (NAMB), one of the United States' largest domestic charities, endeavored to refocus itself around one central mission: to push back lostness in North America through evangelistic church planting. This was a seemingly impossible task, considering that NAMB is more than 160 years old and has dozens of different types of ministries.

The strategy that was begun in 2010 is called Send North America. The goal of the strategy is to see churches planted at a rate faster than the population is growing (something that has not happened since pre-WWI). In order for this strategy to take root, it has meant the sacrifice of hundreds of people. Our partners had to refine their strategies and budgets to come around these new priorities. Our staff had to shift their functions in order to implement the strategy.

At the end of the day, these sacrifices and changes have been necessary so that thousands of churches can be planted and most important, millions of people hear the gospel of Jesus.

Though every person who played a role in this book cannot be named, a few must be mentioned, because without them, the words on these pages and the Send North America strategy would not be a reality.

NAMB Team Members & Partners. You helped develop and refine the ideas that eventually became *Life on Mission.* Steve Canter, Chad Childress, Greg Murphree, Randy Ferguson, Steve Kersh, Ken Miller, Mike Riggins, Shane Critser, Ryan West, Alvin Reid, and Jimmy Scroggins: thank you.

Brandon Clements. Without your ongoing development of the content, writing, and editing over the long haul, this book would have never been inked. You made this book happen—start to finish.

Ginger Kolbaba. Thank you for your help in the editorial shaping of this book into its final form, while providing the encouragement and humor needed in the ninth hour of our deadlines.

Our staff, friends, and publisher. You have read over manuscripts, inspired ideas, modeled the book's DNA, sacrificed a great deal, and picked up the slack in other areas so that this work could be completed. Pat McCarty, Heather Buck, Darby Hanevich, Adam Miller, Micah Millican, Andrew Kistler, Carmon Keith, Beverly Cooper, the crew at Midtown Columbia who live out this DNA, and our new friends at Moody Publishers: Duane Sherman, Parker Hathaway, and Brandon O'Brien.

NAMB Senior Leadership Team. You have been in the trenches tirelessly strategizing, negotiating, and implementing the Send North America strategy. Steve Davis, Jeff Christopherson, Steve Bass, Gary Frost, Carlos Ferrer, Mike Ebert, Clark Logan, and Al Gilbert.

Kevin Ezell (NAMB President). Thank you for fearlessly leading NAMB to a new day. Without your visionary leadership and winsome style, this mission would not be where it is today.

To the people of the Southern Baptist Convention who support the work of North American missions with passion, zeal, and sacrifice. Thank you.

AARON'S PERSONAL ACKNOWLEDGMENTS

To my family for your continual support along this journey to make the name of Jesus famous across North America and the great cities of this world: Carmen, Ezra, Ella, Joshua, and Harper.

DUSTIN'S PERSONAL ACKNOWLEDGMENTS

To my family for the continued encouragement and sacrifice you give toward this work. My greatest joy is living on mission side by side with my favorite mission team: Renie, Jack, and Piper. To Ma, Pa, Mandy, and Wendy for displaying to me a lifetime of what it looks like to faithfully follow Jesus. I am blessed.

Introducing the all new

SEND >> NETWORK

For Church Planters | Church Leaders | Everyday Missionaries

BLOGS VIDEOS EBOOKS EVENTS

Contributors:
Danny Akin, Kevin Ezell, J.D. Greear,
Dhati Lewis, Tony Merida, Thom Rainer,
Paul Tripp, Trevin Wax & more

sendnetwork.com